MArch GAD

Graduate Architectural Design
2012-2013

**The Bartlett
School of Architecture
UCL**

B-Pro

B-Pro, Bartlett Prospective, is a new global postgraduate entity within the School of Architecture currently composed of two courses: MArch Graduate Architectural Design (GAD), an advanced programme led by Alisa Andrasek (Biothing), providing access to the most sophisticated research in design and fabrication; and MArch Urban Design (UD), led by Adrian Lahoud, an advanced programme open to critical and theoretical strategies in urbanism and offering new approaches to planning cities.

The one-year B-Pro programmes are open to a diverse international student cohort and offer highly structured access to the realisation and application of research, and to the production of new schemes of conception and construction in architecture and urbanism. Housed in the School's newly acquired Royal Ear Hospital building, B-Pro has developed numerous lectures, seminars and workshops to underpin these ideas and promote a broad dialogue.

To this end, the 2012-2013 MArch GAD course was organised around eight Research Clusters driven by their respective tutors. These Clusters featured specific research in a number of domains, and offered the opportunity to gain access to new computational tools and a new culture of scripting, directly connected to tools of fabrication. Inspired by, and directly related to, the current scene of international architecture creation, the teaching of software packages such as Maya, Grasshopper, Arduino, Processing and other generative platforms comes from the perspective of an innovative idea of conception and fabrication in association with new digital production facilities (robots, SLS printing, advanced CNC tools etc).

Based on a global overview of the Mediterranean context, the 2012-2013 MArch UD course offered new theoretical schemes to analyse this complex social, cultural, economical and political territory, each of the seven Clusters of the MArch UD working on a specific city (Algiers, Athens, Beirut, Marseille, Messina & Reggio Calabria, Tangier, Tunis). Alternative proposals based on new morphological concepts and protocols were developed in response to urban field studies.

The Bartlett International Lecture Series – with numerous speakers, architects, historians and theoreticians – presented the opportunity for students to be confronted by the main streams of research that will be influential in the near future. Students' work evolved through different crit sessions and the final exhibition in the Royal Ear Hospital, with the presentation of drawings, models and animations, all of a very high quality, which clearly demonstrate the intense activity undertaken throughout the year.

Through the federative idea of creative architecture, B-Pro is an opportunity for students to find a way to participate in a new community and to affirm the singularity and originality of individual talents. These programmes are not only an open door to advanced architecture but also the base from which each student can define a singular practice and invent a strategy to find a position in the professional world.

From 2013, B-Pro will incorporate the MA in the History and Theory of Architecture, to create a larger field of research in theory and to stimulate new exchanges between the three poles of the programme. The school's production facilities will be enhanced with B-Made, a global entity for fabrication which launched in 2013, and the opening of a real factory space.

The 2013 B-Pro exhibition and the publication of this book provide an excellent overview of the depth of quality and the intensity of the teaching of The Bartlett's tutors. What they also showcase is the passion of all the students involved.

Frédéric Migayrou
Bartlett Professor of Architecture
Director of B-Pro

MArch Graduate Architectural Design

The Masters programme in Graduate Architectural Design (GAD) is a 12-month full-time post-professional course, leading to a Masters of Architecture (MArch) degree. The programme is structured around eight Research Clusters curated to deliver diverse yet focused strands of speculative research, emphasising the importance of advanced design in complexities of acute context.

Design plays a key role in the accelerated convergence of matter and information. While data visualisation exposes the hidden beauty, and complexity of observed systems, data materialisation can produce such beauty and complexity within new synthetic fields. The boundaries of disciplines are increasingly porous, giving architecture and design an expanded agency at the centre of open synthesis applicable to a myriad of complex domains.

GAD addresses the adaptation and enrichment of local cultures, complex natural and constructed environments, and active rethinking of design as an extended ecology. The programme recognises the synthetic power of design at the core of complex ecologies, and its ability to bind a plethora of agencies.

Through computational resources, architects have increased access to the physics of materials and structures at different orders of scale. These physics of matter are embedded in the design-search process, incorporating the constraints and inputs of manufacturing and constructability. Research Clusters explore the latest approaches to robotics, computational physics and simulation, generative design, interactivity, advanced algorithms, extensive material experiments and links to material science. GAD engages critically with such developments, which are already radically changing the landscape of architecture, its social and economical role and its effectiveness as an active agency particularly within urban ecologies.

The programme is structured so that students are introduced to theoretical concepts through lectures and initial design projects, supported by computational and robotics skill building workshops. During the second stage, students work in small teams or individually, according to the methodology of each Cluster, allowing the student to focus on their individual interests in advanced design research and the development of a design project. There is a continuous evaluation of work via tutorials with regular design reviews organised between Clusters which include external critics.

Alongside cutting edge research, GAD hosts a series of public events, which this year included the 'Material Matters' and 'Effective Knowledge' lecture series, the Nexus Project and the 'n_Salon', and played host to Smartgeometry 2013. Apart from in-house events open to the larger community, the exceptional pool of the GAD faculty includes some of the most prominent young practitioners and researchers in the field and beyond.

Alisa Andrasek
Programme Leader

Contents

RC4 field trip to Paris, visit to the
Stade Jean-Bouin by Rudy Ricciotti

RC2 visit to Quebec City's Winter Carnival

RC3 at EISCAT in Norway

RC3 expedition to the Arctic Circle

RC4 field trip to Paris, visit to the site of the Fondation Jérôme Seydoux-Pathé by Renzo Piano

Smartgeometry 2013 at The Bartlett

RC7 students in Hong Kong

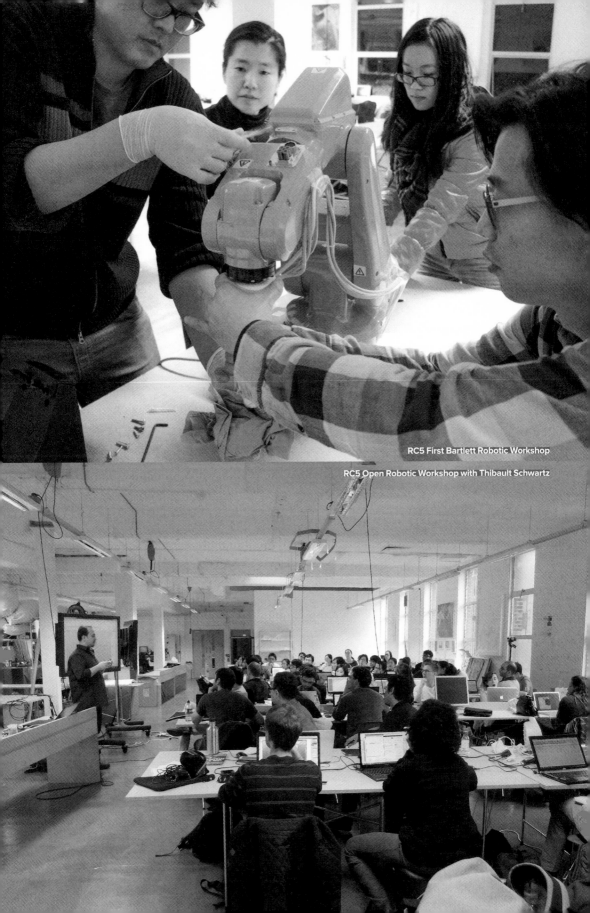

RC5 First Bartlett Robotic Workshop

RC5 Open Robotic Workshop with Thibault Schwartz

Research
Cluster

1

Synthetic Constructability: Increased Resolution Fabric of Architecture

Alisa Andrasek with Daghan Cam and Maj Plemenitas

The Bartlett School of Architecture 2013

The recent arrival of extreme volumes of computation, finer grains of computational physics deployed through simulations, highly resilient Multi-Agent Systems (MAS) and large data sourced from a myriad of material and immaterial domains are opening new spaces of synthesis for architecture. Research Cluster 1 explores the activation of robotics in convergence with computational physics and MAS towards innovative constructability in order to research new and increased resolution fabric of architecture. A thick materiality of abstraction (via computational families such as CA, MAS, fluid dynamics and similar) was bound by the constraints of production and material research. Synthetic design/production ecologies result in proposals for the plastic yet mutable fabric of architecture, with various new 'superpowers' that were not possible with the previous resolution of structure and matter. Such fabric opens the potential for non-anthropocentric agency in design. One particular class of agency is connected with universal non-local properties, using physics as the building blocks of architecture. This architecture draws on large data from the finer-grain physics of matter – matter as information, enabled by computation. These tendencies do not only expand on technically enriched material formations, but also activate previously hidden material powers towards designs beyond our anticipations in both formal imagination and performance. A new speculative image of matter reveals things beyond the established concepts of 'nature' – via matter as information, matter as an active agency, matter as strange and unnatural. Finer grain physics simulations disrupt the blueprints of architecture, resulting in structures with increased resiliency, plasticity and malleability of complex interrelated systems – in short, increased design-ability within complex ecologies. This allows for speculative proposals of unprecedented nature, complexity, intricacy and scale.

The four research projects developed within the Cluster range from topics such as the interplay of noise sourced from the material behaviours of expandable foam, and pseudo noise sourced from vestiges of computational time, across extreme resolutions of building blocks organised through robotic deposition and packing geometries, via swarms for distributed robotic braiding of space filling structures or the weaving of spanning structures with robotic arms. RoboFoam looked at the increasingly expanding category of foam-based materials and engaged with ubiquitous expandable foam used for thermal insulation in conventional construction, characterised by a high degree of non-linearity. The capacities of this material were extended by the introduction of the extreme precision of algorithmic and robotic production. MAS and computational physics simulations were employed and woven into a design space. Aesthetic, thermal and structural capacities are mined from the interplay of noice and accuracy. In Crystal Cloud, students researched the intricate transmission of light and its reflection/refraction achieved through the robotic deposition of very fine building blocks. In spherical packing, materials such as glass, marble and synthetic composites are used, as well as the robotic injection of high performance binding veins – programed through the scanning of adaptive MAS.

Further speculations are made for the future construction of precisely deposited multi-materials within large scale building structures. In the Fluid Weaving project, unnatural physics of liquids generated through programmable computational time were used as a form-finding resource. Through a series of algorithmically driven structural relaxation procedures, woven patterns were developed for such extremely intricate, lightweight and large span structures, that were then fed as data streams into a robotic arm for high precision weaving. The blueprints of such structures look more like interwoven galaxies than classical architectural drawings. Finally, in Robotic Braiding, complex adaptive behaviours frequently found in biology, such as the collective organisation of flocks of birds and schools of fish were materialised as a model for

constructability through distributed robotics.
An algorithmically trained, robotically enabled
swarm of vehicles performs the multithreaded
weaving of intricate spatial fabrics. Recent
developments in fibres and new high-performance
materials can help us envision high performance
structures, whereby different fibres of architectural
fabrics such as infrastructural elements (light, energy
storage and transmission, multicoloured patterns
and similar) can be interwoven into a superstructure.
The project was presented at Tsinghua University in
Beijing and Tongji University in Shanghai.

Students
Shahad Al Hadeethi, Elina Christou, Jan (Ian)
Dierckx, Tianran (Tina) Dong, Shuwei (Vincent) Hao,
Amirreza Mirmotahari, Rodrigo Novelo Pastrana,
Nikola Papic, Shuo Qian, Jing Jun Tao, Ioanna
Theodosiou, Mo Wang, Tianqi (Alex) Wang,
Shengchen Yang

Project teams
Crystal Cloud Amirreza Mirmotahari, Ioanna
Theodosiou, Shahad Al Hadeethi
Fluid Tianran Dong, Shuwei Hao, Shuo Qian,
Jing Jun Tao
RoboFoam Elina Christou, Jan (Ian) Dierckx,
Rodrigo Novelo Pastrana, Nikola Papic
Robotic Braiding Mo Wang, Tianqi (Alex) Wang,
Shengchen Yang

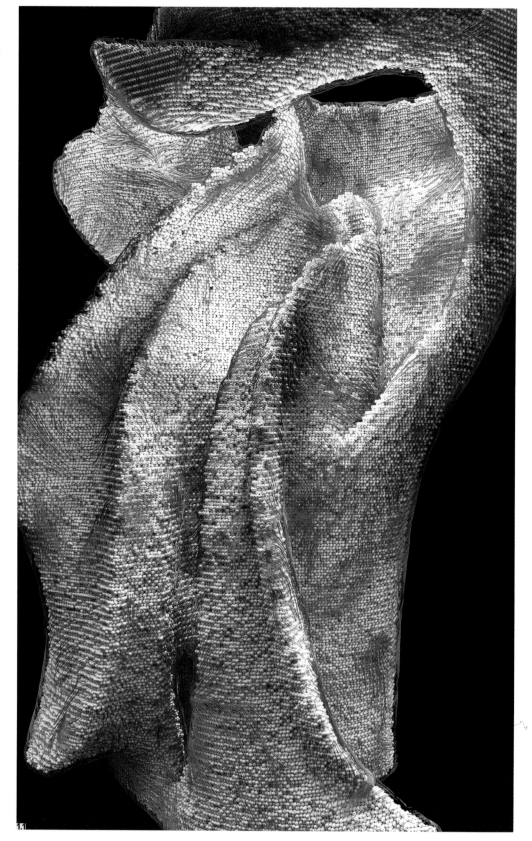

1.1

1.2

1.1 – 1.6 Crystal Cloud 1.1 The storm formation is considered to be the first layer of data distribution in space in global scale. Air dynamics are used to achieve intricate formations with billions of particles and manipulate future design approaches. **1.2** Section of a large scalestructural assembly that captures light in itself and brings it to the underworld. The veins represent structure reinforcing agents which are transparent in the final artefacts.

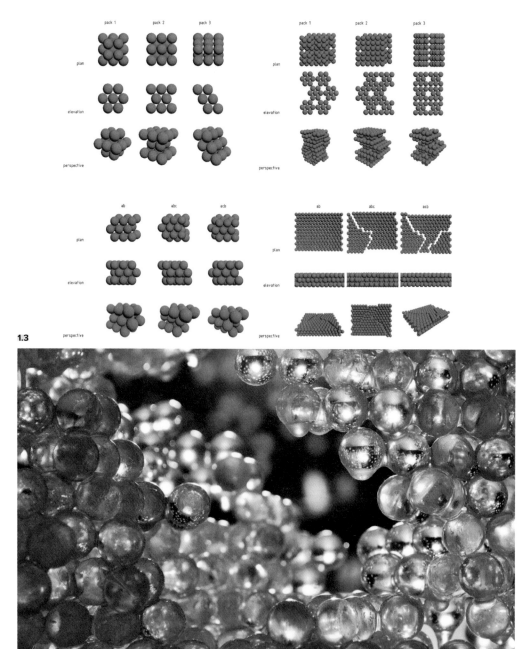

1.3

1.4

1.3 Initial studies into how sphere packing patterns could be used in order to achieve different textures and stable structures. **1.4** Physical model fabricated as part of a simulation and analysed in the skydome environment at The Bartlett. Different qualities of light filtration, reflection, and refraction are dependent on the distribution and amount of matter. **1.5** Final design proposal for the new entrance of V&A Museum. A labyrinthine pre-entrance gallery, in which one gets lost and experiences different light phenomena that guides one through space. **1.6** Elevation sequences of the structural formation.

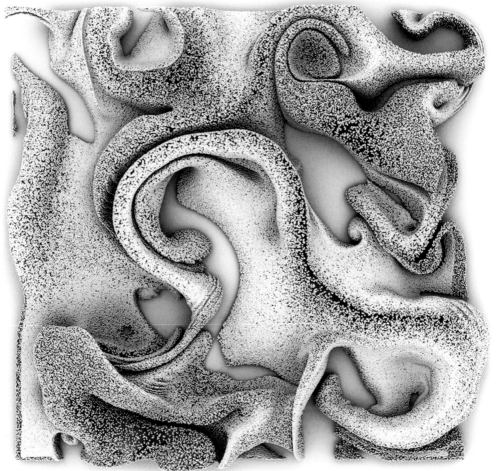

1.5

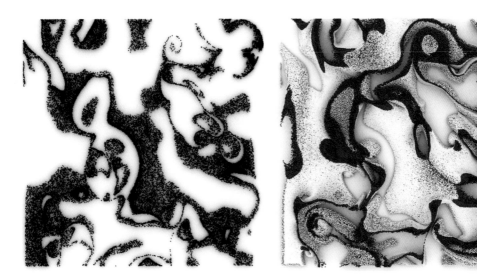

1.6

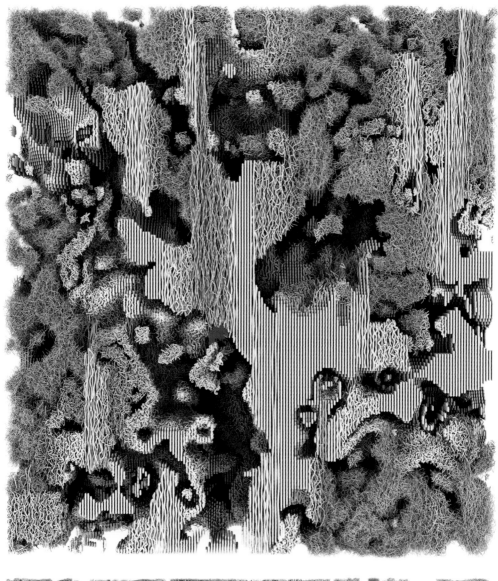

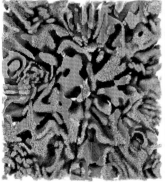 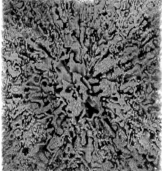 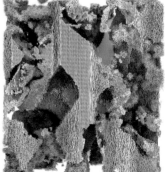

1.7

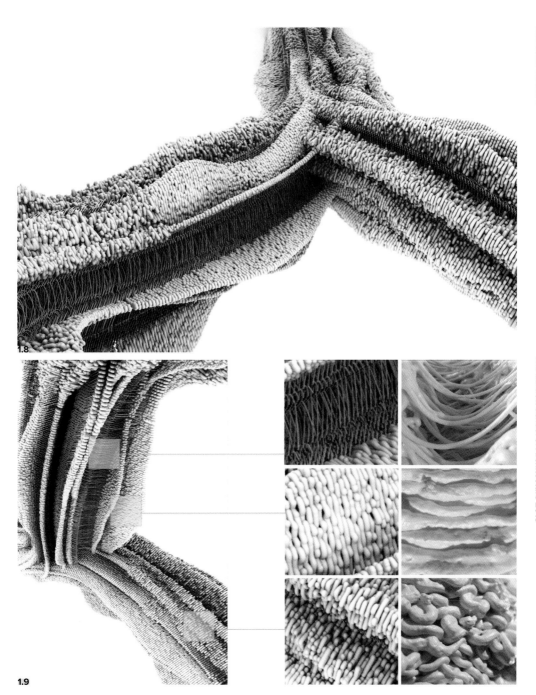

1.8

1.9

1.7 – 1.12 RoboFoam 1.7 Space formation studies leading
to the generation of a high-resolution fabric of architecture.
1.8 Material noise articulation study for an atypical column.
1.9 Comparison between digital and physical material
behaviour.

1.10

1.11

1.12

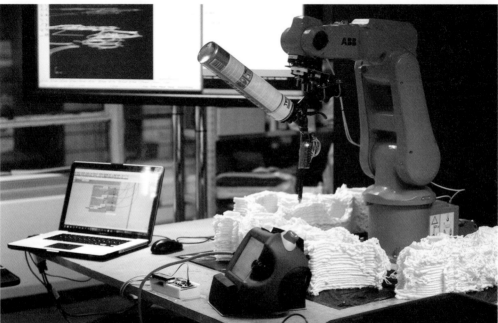

1.13

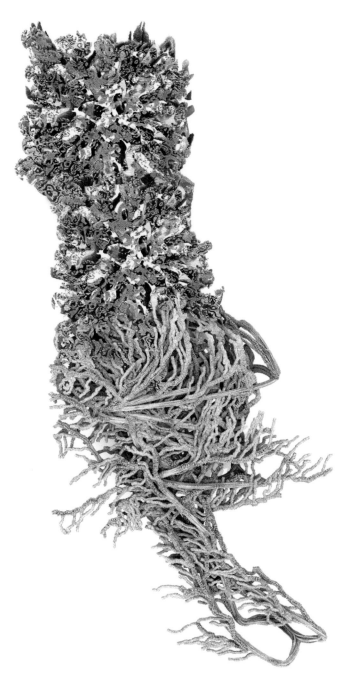

1.14

1.10 – 1.11 Robotic manufactured foam physical models.
1.12 Comparison between digital and physical material
behaviour. **1.13** Robotic fabrication process. **1.14** Material noise
articulation compaison between simulation and foam physical
model.

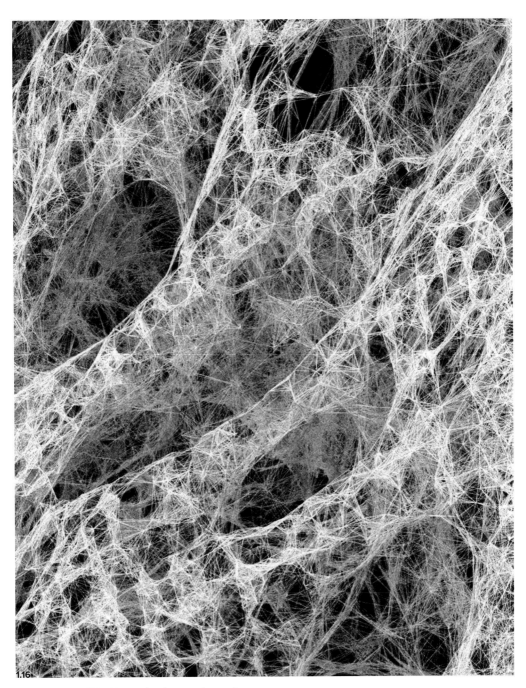

1.16

1.15 – 1.22 Fluid 1.15 Highly articulated structural network
formation. **1.16** Detail of the structural network.

1.18

1.17 Digital simulation for the fluid dynamic project. The investigation of liquid behaviour is the aim of this simulation as part of the greater project. The result is a specific motion path sculpture that is created during the human dance. **1.18** The motion of the liquid is characterised by the changing speed of the body, an element of the behaviour that we were interested in. When the speed is higher, the structure becomes unstable in combination with splash shells and when the speed is lower the structure becomes more stable. **1.19** The structure resulting from a fluid dynamic model is created by the different behaviours of liquid emerging from the constantly changing speed which has a vital role in the project. **1.20** Internal force distribution simulation.

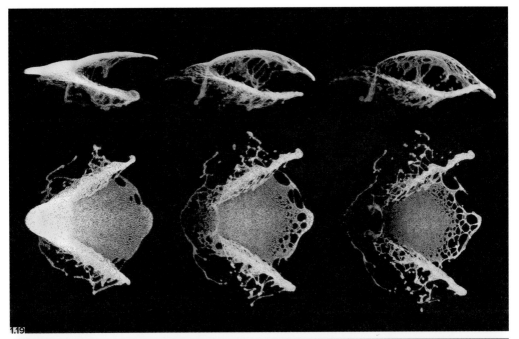

1.19

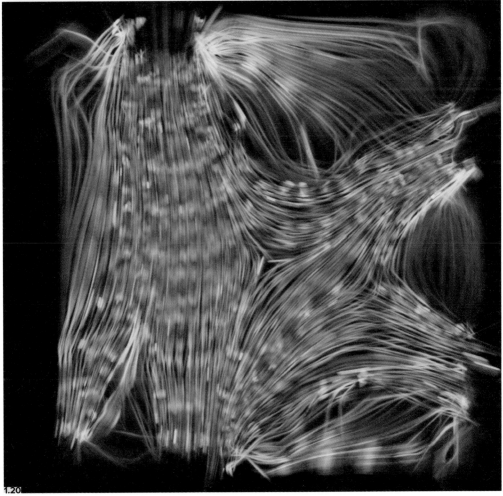

1.20

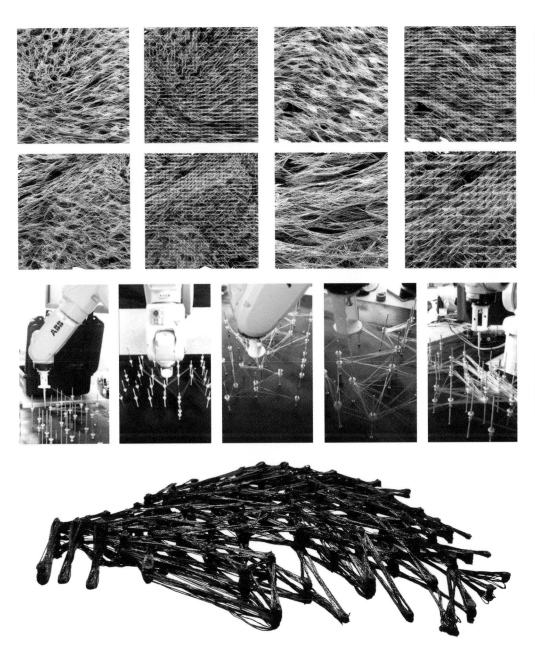

1.22

1.21 Network with variable articulated density and directionality conditions. **1.22** Materialisation process. Precisely controlled robotic fibre placement. **1.23 RoboBraiding** The elevation of the column reveals not only the evolution of the structure, but local detail texture and intricacy as well. Rendering shows internal space and detail of adhesion.

The Bartlett School of Architecture 2013

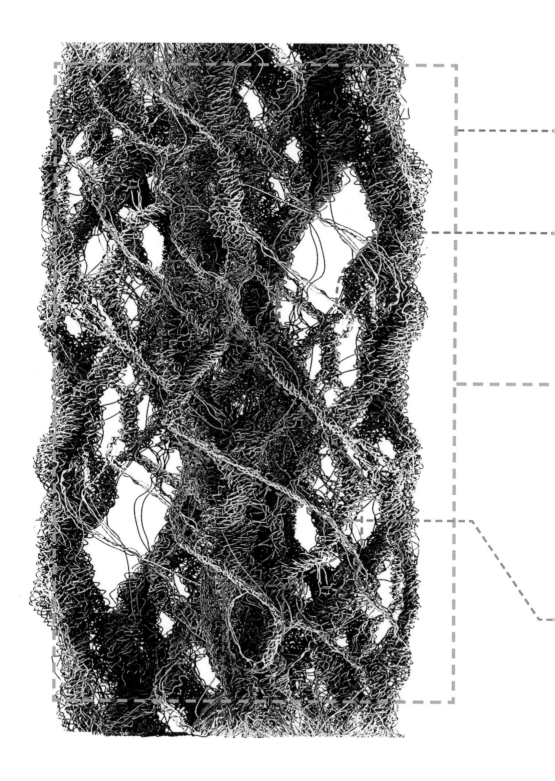

1.23

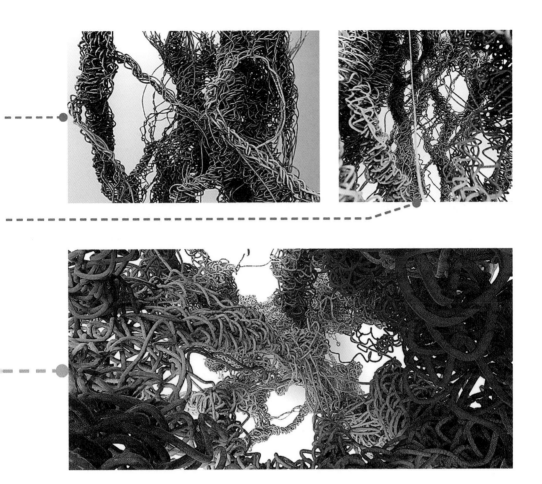

1.24

1.25

1.26

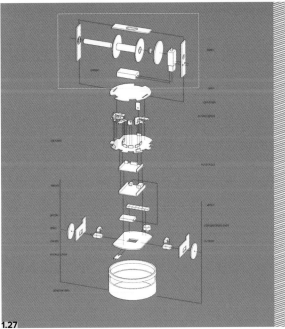

1.27

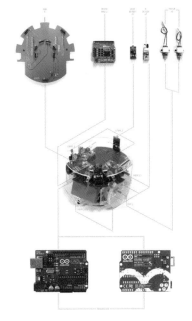

1.24 RoboBraiding A choreography of distributed mobile bots. Light sensors are built into B-BOT so that it can respond to light environments. The robots swarm on the ground and braid the structure. **1.25** Swarm of B-BOTS. **1.26** 30 mobile robots were built and code was written to control their behaviours. **1.27** Diagram showing mechanical components and the electronic circuit plan.

Research
Cluster

OPALESCENCE, TRANSLUCENCY etc.

Marjan Colletti and Pavlos Fereos with Guan Lee

Research: Qualities

What are the criteria by which we can discuss and evaluate the performativity and poetics of materiality in architecture? Research Cluster 2 looked at:

Mind-independent **parameters**, with extensive and extensive attributes, which represent the 'direct measurements of a building, that is of its spaces, the architectural activities it accommodates, and of the consumers involved.' (M. R. Savchenko)

User-centric **properties** – reactions and emotions – the 'indirect measurements' of different readings, meanings and reactions inferred by an 'intermediary' consumer (user) 'who enters into the "make-up" of the actual buildings'; some overlaid 'symbolic situations'. (M. R. Savchenko)

Capacities: open-ended interactions and interrelations with other material bodies. Compared to 'finite in number and always given' properties, capacities are 'potential and potentially open-ended' and hence 'always relational'. That is, a 'capacity may exist virtually and may never be exercised, and if yes, then it could only be exercised in relationship to another material body. For example: a knife's capacity is to cut, and cutting can only happen if something else is being cut.' (M. DeLanda)

Tendencies: the possibility of variation, adaptability and change, 'properties are also subject to tendencies. The tendency of material entities at certain critical points of a condition allows a change from one set of properties to another.' (M. DeLanda)

Effects, caused by agencies and more 'visceral than intellectual, more atmospheric than aesthetic' impressions. (J Kipnis)

Affects on the other hand refer to symptoms, to emotional changes. (J Kipnis)

Haecceities: the discrete qualities, properties or characteristics of a thing which make it particular.

Of most interest to us are **phenomena**, embedded within a feedback system of events and observations. They involve a wide set of scientific and strategic rules and values but also spatio-temporal coincidences.

Design: Archiglace
Inclusions

RC2 and students from the University of Waterloo created an ice structure/enclosure for the Musée National Des Beaux-Arts du Québec during the annual Winter Carnival in Quebec City. The primary material is water/ice. Each team introduced one or more secondary materials to be included in the formation of this structure. The challenge was to determine both how and when the integrations would occur to achieve the desired outcome.

'Inclusion' is a term used in metallurgy to refer to materials that are trapped inside a mineral during its formation. Brittle, transparent, colourless, and crystalline, ice as a mineral can be immensely versatile. Fluid like its antecedent, it is radiant in opalescence when light passes through it. An inclusion can be read as an impurity or defect. However, in this project we asked whether inclusions could rather be conceived as opportunities for new structures. Can minerals grow organically like plants? Can a system of structure make itself? The average temperature in Quebec City in February is around -12 degrees Celsius: a drop of water exposed to the environment may become solid in an instant. If a network of flexible and slight materials are sprayed with water, they can become rigid and load-bearing when water freezes around them. Working with inclusions, RC2 explored whether the embedded object can act like a scaffold for water to travel on, a guide for crystals of ice to form and develop into an edifice that is not predetermined. The resulting structure is the product of experiments in which hybridity informs the strategic process in design. The aim was to explore a process-based design investigation with an icy flesh but bearing at its core a series of inclusions. Water/ice can be shaped not just by its container but also by how it is manoeuvred. Assisted growth is neither an additive nor a subtractive process, but an opportunistic pursuit of dynamic interactions, as materials form in their environment.

Musée de Glace

Current design preoccupations with form generation through digital means often overlook the necessary relationship to material realities, place and nature. ArchiGlace for example calls for a close examination of a particular material formation, ice. The emphasis is not just on the final solid state of the ice architecture but also on the process and environment that facilitate the outcome. The Musée de Glace is an architectural proposal set for construction in winter 2014, marking a decade after The Snow Show, in which seventeen leading architects were paired with internationally renowned artists to build with ice or snow. The structures resulting from this exhibition in Lapland, Finland were not simply about ice as a substance but crucially they engaged with issues of light, space and temporality. Ten years on, RC2 will investigate how new digital fabrication techniques can be employed in construction with ice. The site of the Musée de Glace is Quebec City, a city known as a snow capital and its historic winter carnival. This design proposal intends to further the explorations, learning and discoveries from ArchiGlace into the realm of inhabitable structures and architecture articulated in the very essence of ice, transparency.

For digital modelling and scripting workshops, we would like to thank Niccolò Casas, Pavlos Fereos, Arthur Mamou-Mani and Marios Tsiliakos.

Our collaborators on Archiglace/Inclusions were Professor Anne Bordeleau and students Justin Breg, Tiffany Chiang, Virginia Fernandez, Emad Ghattas, Danielle Gignac, Miriam Ho, Taeh Yung Kim, Henry Murdock, Shane Neill, Connor O'Grady, Samantha Oswald and May Wu from the University of Waterloo.

Students
Shuchi Agarwal, Cindy Charisa , Kai Li, Xiaoxu Li, François Mangion, Maria-Silena Patsalidou, Dimitra Poulokefalou, Zachary Saunders, Rukmani Thangam, Eleftheria Varda, Dali Xu, Ran Yan, Ali Zolfaghari

Project teams
Team Crystal
Bartlett: Cindy Charisa, Maria-Silena Patsalidou, Dimitra Poulokefalou, Rukmani Thangam
Waterloo: Taeh Yung Kim, Samantha Oswald, Danielle Gignac
Team Lemon
Bartlett: Zachary Saunders, Eleftheria Varda
Waterloo: Miriam Ho, Henry Murdock
Team Splash
Bartlett: Kai Li, Xiaoxu Li, Dali Xu
Waterloo: Tiffany Chiang, Virginia Fernandez, Shane Neill
Team Caustic
Bartlett: François Mangion, Shuchi Agarwal, Ran Yan, Ali Zolfaghari
Waterloo: Connor O'Grady, Emad Ghattas, May Wu, Justin Breg

2.1

2.1 – 2.3 Archiglace/Inclusions These ice installations were exhibited at the Musée National Des Beaux-Arts du Québec during the annual Winter Carnival in Quebec City, Canada. Archiglace/Inclusions was created in collaboration with the University of Waterloo. Students worked together in four teams. **2.1 Team Crystal** Laser-cut watercolour paper and plastic sheets were interlocked together to form an aggregated cloud then sprayed with water at -20°C. **2.2 Team Lemon** Loose-woven gauze-like cotton fabric sheets were laser cut and manually manipulated before they were sprayed with water to form wall panels for a small enclosure. **2.3 Team Splash** Multiples of silicone moulds were created to cast in ice more than 65 single identical/repeated elements that could be welded together to form a screen wall.

2.2

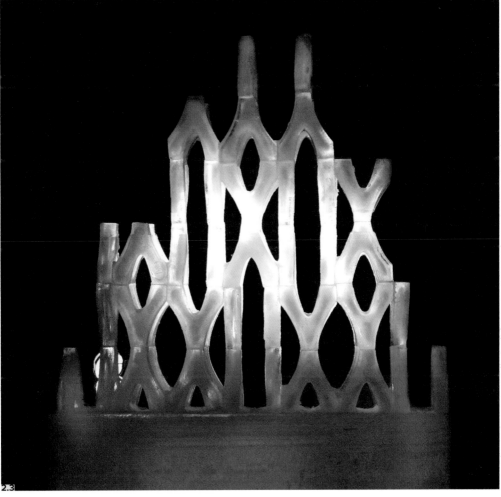

2.3

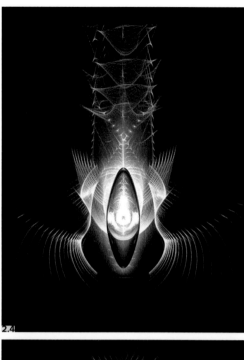

2.4

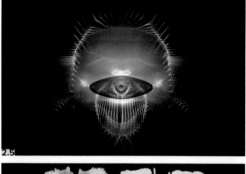

2.5

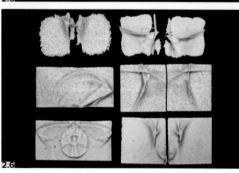

2.6

2.7

2.4 – 2.7 Shuchi Agarwal, François Mangion 2.4 – 2.5 Images created with simulations of caustic pattern and light caustic analysis through transparent geometric objects. Digital renderings. **2.6** Pâte de verre, glass fabrication of surfaces generated through caustic curves. Granular recycled glass. **2.7** Caustic based and digitally fabricated surface design. Backlit CNC milled acrylic sheet. **2.8 Xiaoxu Li, Ran Yan** Glass wax experiments. Cotton strings are first dipped into a container of melted glass wax, as the container slowly pulls away from the strings, the glass wax is stretched/formed as the glass wax solidifies. The rate of the moving container is timed with the rate of the glass wax turning solid.

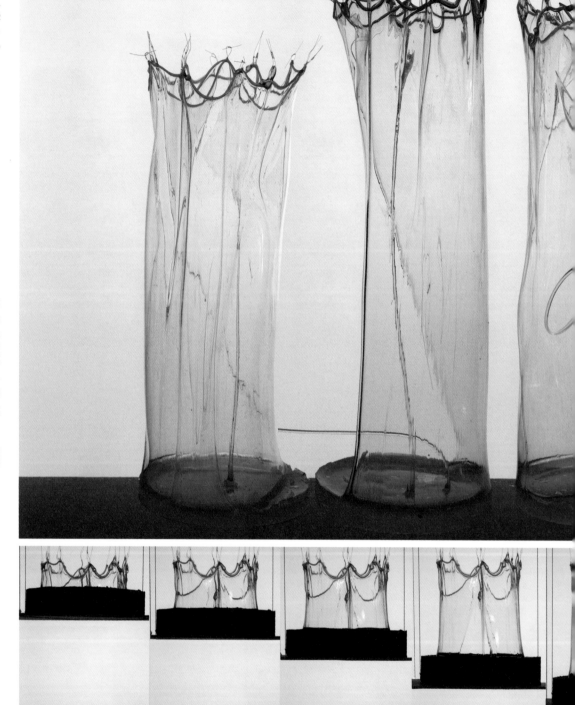

2.8

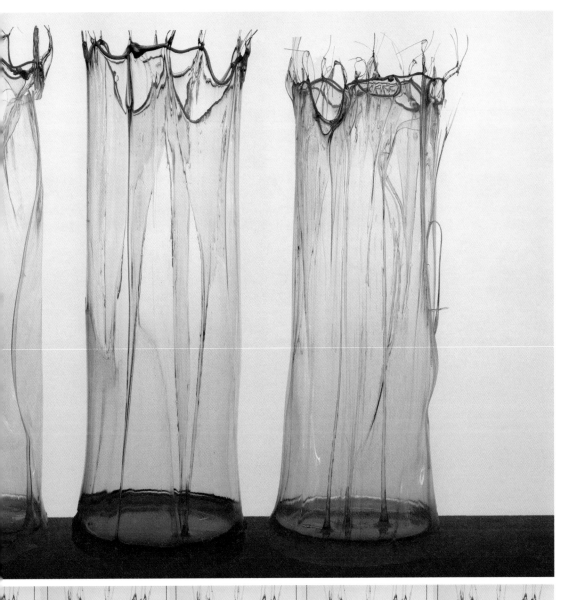

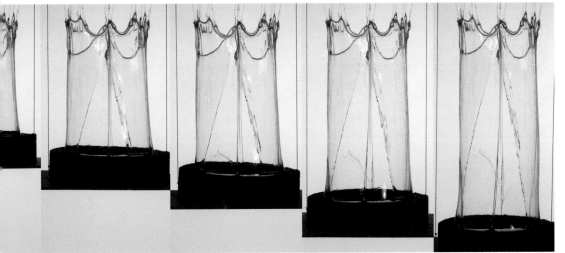

2.9

2.9 – 2.10 Maria-Silena Patsalidou, Dimitra Poulokefalou
Digital Scaffolding/Inhabiting the waterfall. **2.9** Front elevation.
Part of this drawing also reveals the interior of the museum,
exhibition spaces and the gardens. Digital rendering.
2.10 Digital Scaffolding/Inhabiting the waterfall. Perspective
view of the building. Digital rendering. **2.11 Cindy Charisa,
Rukmani Thangam** An Architecture of Ephemerality. This
building exploits the temporal nature of ice, creating a visually
and spatially dynamic experience. Digital rendering.

2.10

2.11

2.12

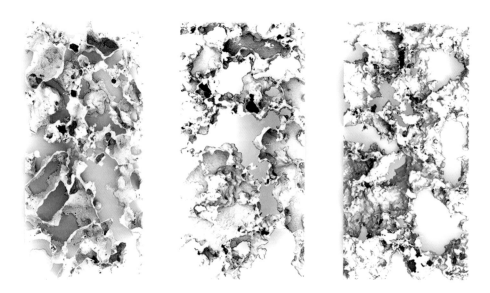

2.13

2.12 – 2.13 Eleftheria Varda ACID Architecture. **2.12** Foam
profile sections – initial form exploration. Digital rendering.
2.13 Digital exploration – internal cave formation. Digital
rendering. **2.14 Zachary Saunders** Toward a Complex Body of
Architecture: Vascular-System_Segment-1. Digital rendering.

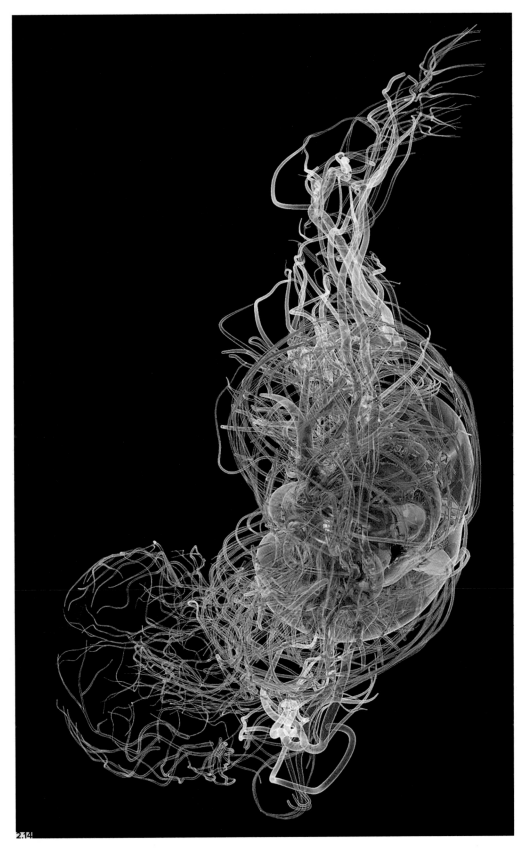

2.14

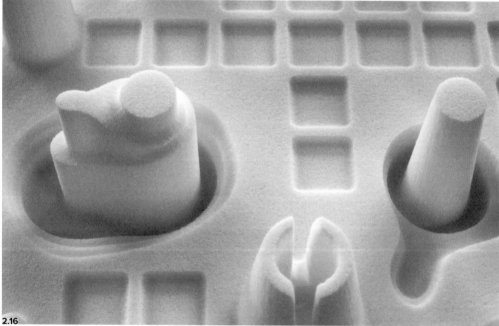

2.15 Ali Zolfaghari Translucency, light, and visual softness are developed through modelling. Laminated Perspex sheets. **2.16 Ali Zolfaghari** Mould for ice structure, elements of nature to form architecture. CNC milled high density foam. **2.17 Dali Xu** Pattern transition (between landscape and structure). Digital rendering. **2.18 Dali Xu** Inverted hanging fabric-structure. Fabric and milled foam model.

2.17

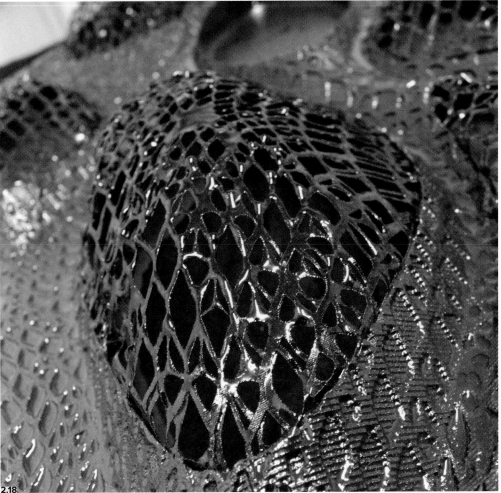

2.18

2.19 – 2.20 Shuchi Agarwal, François Mangion Synaesthetic
Museum **2.19** Internal view. Digital rendering. **2.20** External
view. Digital rendering.

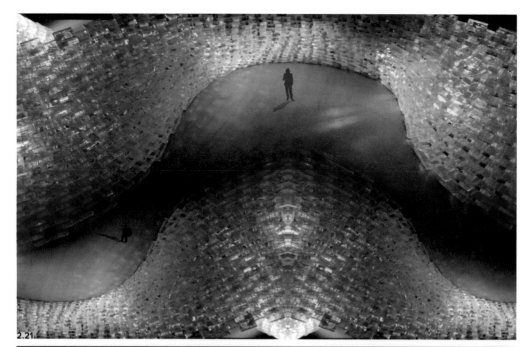

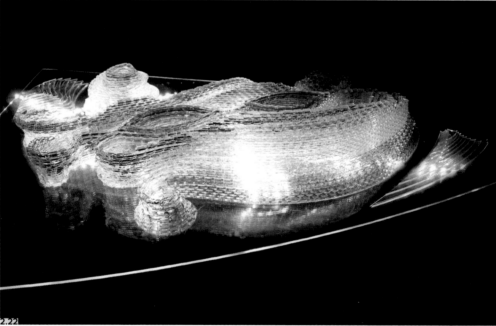

2.21 – 2.22 Kai Li The Streamlined Light. This ice museum located in Quebec City aims to explore the potential of brick vortex-structure, a dynamic indoor and outdoor environment. **2.21** Space between two curved walls made of transparent ice bricks. Perspex model. **2.22** Perspex model. **2.23 Shuchi Agarwal, François Mangion** Caustic ray-tracing analysis of changing water surface using directional light source. Digital rendering.

Research
Cluster

Motive Mythologies

Ruairi Glynn, Ollie Palmer

The Bartlett School of Architecture 2013

Motive
1. In motion or transformation
2. Having reason for action

Mythology
1. Chronicle of a religious or cultural tradition
2. Belief about a person, thing, place, or situation, exaggerated or fictitious

Humankind seeks out novelty and finds pleasure in engaging that which is ambiguous, or contradicts its present state of knowing. In coming to terms with something new, we conceptualise and abstract in order to solve problems and ultimately take greater control. This imperative motivates our social desires to communicate, and interact with the world around us. Patterns are sought to be found between new encounters and a history of experiences, some we accumulate ourselves, others neuro-science suggests we are born 'hardwired' with.

We have spent this past year understanding how patterns of motion and transformation found in our natural world viscerally guide our imagination, our mythologies, our rituals, artefacts and artifice. From our field trip to Mexico we discovered that according to Mesoamerican Mythology, there have been four historical ages, called Suns – those of earth, wind, fire and water. Each has been destroyed. The era of the Sun of Movement which began on 11 August 3114 BCE is estimated to have ended on 21 December 2012 after a period of 5126 years.

We now enter the Time of the Sixth Sun, predicted in the Mesoamerican calendar as a time of transformation and the creation of new race. Whether you wish to believe this prophecy, undoubtedly bio/nano/info-technologies are forging radical transformations in our relationship to our natural and built environment. The question of how we as architects take a role in designing, engineering and fabricating these new active, reactive, interactive spaces is one the Cluster continues to question.

Through 1:1 prototyping we have designed and fabricated motive objects and installations exploring novel interactions, performance, mythologies, and speculative futures. Our research has been inherently time-based, characterised in three distinct conceptual modes which formed the basis of the three terms of project development:

Term 1
Automatic: single choreographed behaviour following a linear arrangement from beginning to end.

Term 2
Reactive: multiple choreographed behaviours following non-linear arrangements, triggered by stimuli.

Term 3
Interactive: un-choreographed behaviours formed through exchanges between participants.

This year we have built kinetic structures that wildly roam Victoria Park, worn prosthetics that test the extreme limits of human bearability, choreographed dances with industrial robots, we've built cyclones and sculpted clouds out of sugar, been hypnotised by our own heartbeat, seen sound shape material, we've stood on the Moon Temple of Tenochtitlan, had an expedition to the Arctic Circle, witnessed and listened to the Aurora Borealis, and performed surreal shadow puppetry in the Tanks at Tate Modern.

We are grateful to our tutors and critics Yota Adilenidou, Alisa Andrasek, Alessandro Ayuso, Paul Bavister, Jason Bruges, Emma Bush, Ben Cerveny, Angelos Chronis, Carole Collet, Marjan Colletti, Regine Debatty, Bernadette Devilat, David Di Duca, Pavlos Fereos, Prof. Stephen Gage, Fred Guttfield, Sean Hanna, Alex Haw, Petros Koutsolampros, Diony Kypraiou, Elie Lakin, Guan Lee, Chris Leung, Lux, Sam McElhinney, Prof. Frédéric Migayrou, Marianne Mulvey, Bakul Patki, Elliot Payne, Luke Pearson, Marco Poletto, Andrew

Porter, Molly Price, Felipe Lanuza Rilling, David Roberts, Richard Roberts, Jose Sanchez, Prof. Bob Sheil, Ben Tew, Theodoros Themistokleous, Martha Tsigkari, Filip Visnjic, Mellissa Woolford and Fiona Zisch. Thanks to our workshop leaders Sam Conran and Emmett Glynn, Ben Haworth and Zoi Karagkiozi, Ryan Mehanna and Theodoros Themistokleous, Ollie Palmer and Stefanie Wuschitz, Catrina Stewart, Hugh McEwen and Alice Labourel, and Fiona Zisch.

Students
William Bondin, Aimilia (Emily) Kritikou, Shichong Li, Yifan (Eva) Liu, Quingling Tan, Chryssa Varna

3.1

3.2

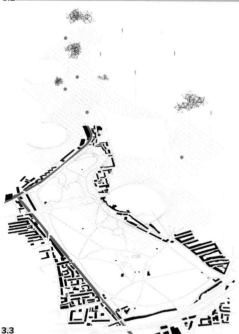

3.3

3.4

3.1 – 3.2 William Bondin Photomontages of Mobile-Reconfigurable-Polyhedra (MORPH) occupying a public park landscape. Following experiments with passive dynamic walkers and research into embodied computation, a proposal for modular walking trusses was developed. These motive trusses encourage user participation through their playful behaviour and persuasive communication. The research addresses a number of issues, including the inherent gap between predicted simulation and actual behaviour in architectural structures. **3.3 William Bondin** Plan for London's Victoria Park to be inhabited by architectural scale walking polyhedra. Different instances of interaction, occupation, navigation and observance are proposed through a multi-layered design computational strategy. An ubiquitous navigation and communication system was inspired by the cognitive mechanism of slime mould. **3.4 William Bondin** Inherent Motives. A prototype of a mobile tetrahedron performing a crawling action. Linear movement across the edges is translated into a radial gait by the structure's morphology and embodied behaviour. Bi-linear actuators developed in collaboration with Paul Harkin.

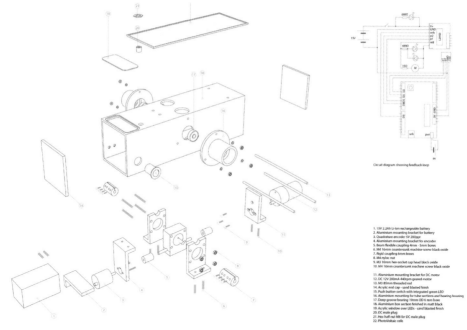

Circuit diagram showing feedback loop

1. 15V 2.2Ah Li-Ion rechargeable battery
2. Aluminium mounting bracket for battery
3. Quadrature encoder 5V 200ppr
4. Aluminium mounting bracket for encoder
5. Beam flexible coupling 4mm - 5mm bores
6. M4 16mm countersunk machine screw black oxide
7. Rigid coupling 6mm bores
8. M4 nyloc nut
9. M3 10mm hex-socket cap head black oxide
10. M4 16mm countersunk machine screw black oxide

11. Aluminium mounting bracket for DC motor
12. DC 12V 200mA 440rpm geared motor
13. M3 85mm threaded rod
14. Acrylic end cap - sand blasted finish
15. Push button switch with integrated green LED
16. Aluminium mounting for tube sections and bearing housing
17. Deep groove bearing 19mm OD 6 mm bore
18. Aluminium box section finished in matt black
19. Acrylic window over LEDs - sand blasted finish
20. DC male plug
21. Hex half nut M8 for DC male plug
22. Photolstaic cells

3.5

3.6

3.5 William Bondin Exploded axonometric view of an iteration of a custom servo-mechanisms designed to animate walking polyhedra. The individual elements contribute to the emergence of a resilient behavioural framework through which the whole structure, in its totality, can perform. **3.6 William Bondin** Assembling and fitting a custom engineered servo-mechanism. **3.7 RC3 Arctic Expedition** Visit to EISCAT, Tromsø, Norway. Students observing Laser Experiments to measure particle density within the earth's higher atmosphere.

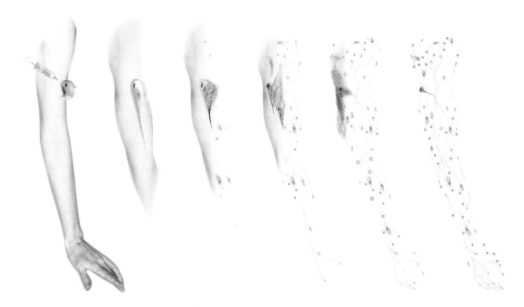

3.8

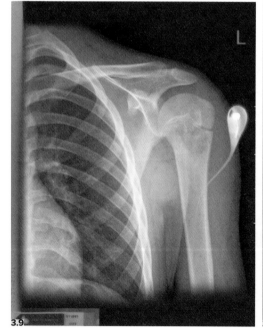

3.9

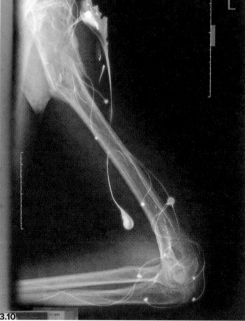

3.10

3.8 – 3.11 Qingling Tan SEED. Created as part of ongoing research into the effect of Mediated Reality on users and their interaction with the built environment, SEED aims to investigate the limits of human bearability to technological prostheses. SEED speculates on a future where embedded prostheses form a symbiotic relationship with the user's body, taking on the DNA and characteristics of the user through a prolonged period of growth and interaction. **3.8** Set of conceptual drawings illustrating the growth of the 'SEED' prosthetic inside a user's body and on the skin through prolonged period of growth and interaction. **3.9** Monthly diagnosis. The user is given monthly updates on their SEED prosthetic in the form of an X-ray diagnosis. This X-ray scan shows the initial growth of the SEED device in the body. **3.10** This X-ray scan shows

the growth of the SEED device after prolonged period of interaction. Signs of crystal formations seen on the device as its user consumes mineral supplements wishing to grow the SEED with the appearance he or she desires. **3.11** Speculative advertisement for the SEED prosthetic. The advertisement seeks to illustrate how packaging could influence consumers into desiring such an invasive device.

CONTROL OF NEGATIVE THOUGHTS; SAY GOODBYE TO UNWANTED AND TROUBLING THOUGHTS! A PERSONAL ORGANISER, MAKES ALL THE RIGHT DECISIONS! ESCAPE FANTASIES AND REALITY MASSAGING; BOREDOM AND ROUTINE INTERRUPTION, PERCEPTION ALTERED! MAKES ANYWHERE FEELS LIKE HOME, BE A STRANGER TO NO-ONE MASTER THE ART OF BEING ALIVE!

SEED
- BEARING THE SEED TO YOUR FUTURE -

3.11

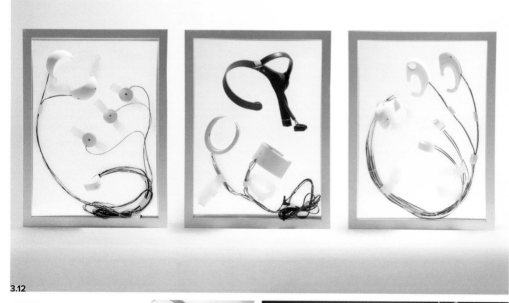

3.12

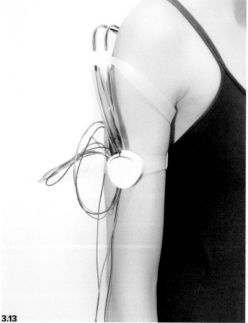

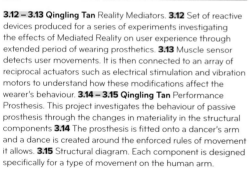

3.13

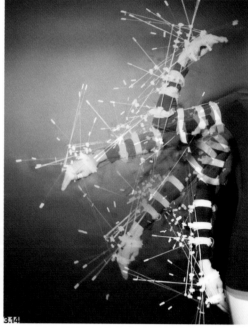

3.14

3.12 – 3.13 Qingling Tan Reality Mediators. **3.12** Set of reactive devices produced for a series of experiments investigating the effects of Mediated Reality on user experience through extended period of wearing prosthetics. **3.13** Muscle sensor detects user movements. It is then connected to an array of reciprocal actuators such as electrical stimulation and vibration motors to understand how these modifications affect the wearer's behaviour. **3.14 – 3.15 Qingling Tan** Performance Prosthesis. This project investigates the behaviour of passive prosthesis through the changes in materiality in the structural components **3.14** The prosthesis is fitted onto a dancer's arm and a dance is created around the enforced rules of movement it allows. **3.15** Structural diagram. Each component is designed specifically for a type of movement on the human arm.

The components are 3D-printed and manually fitted with silicone elements to have rigid and flexible performance in strategic areas.

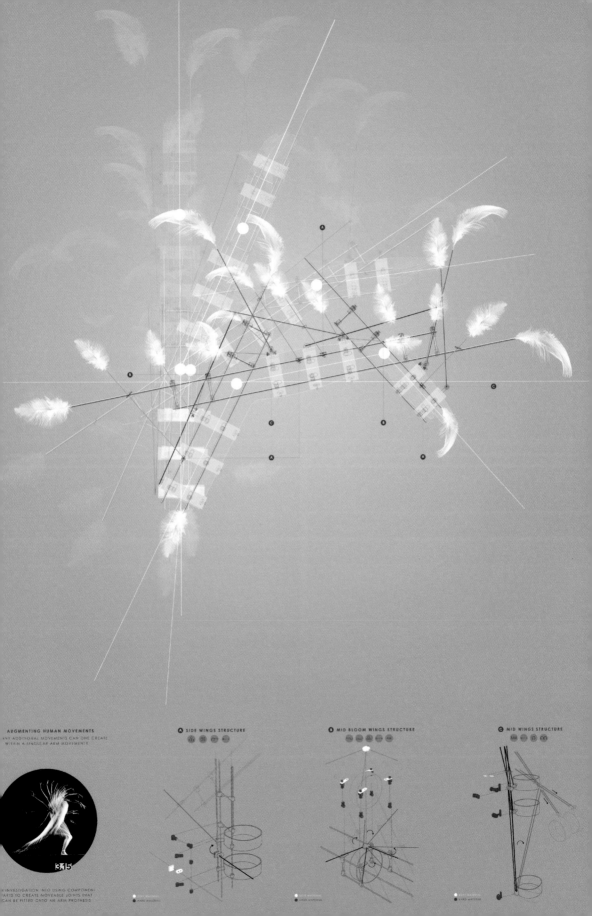

AUGMENTING HUMAN MOVEMENTS

ANY ADDITIONAL MOVEMENTS CAN ONE CREATE
WITHIN A SINGULAR ARM MOVEMENT?

A SIDE WINGS STRUCTURE

B MID BLOOM WINGS STRUCTURE

C MID WINGS STRUCTURE

AN INVESTIGATION INTO USING COMPONENT
PARTS TO CREATE MOVEABLE JOINTS THAT
CAN BE FITTED ONTO AN ARM PROTHESIS

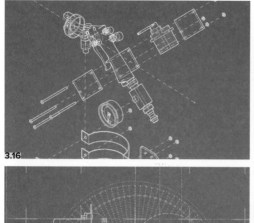

3.16

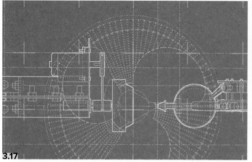

3.17

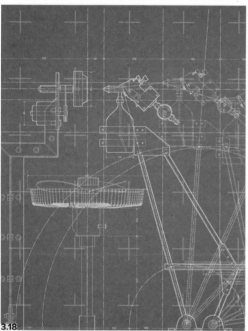

3.18

3.19

3.16 – 3.19 **Shichong Li** Cloud Sculptor. **3.16 – 3.18** Detailed blueprints of the mechanical operations that actuate his sugary weather machine. **3.19** Shichong Li stands beside his purpose built Candy Cloud Cyclone Chamber watching a sweet accumulation form in mid-air. Carefully controlling temperture of sugar and airflow, his mission continues to build a candy cloud big enough to compete with its watery brothers in the skyline of London.

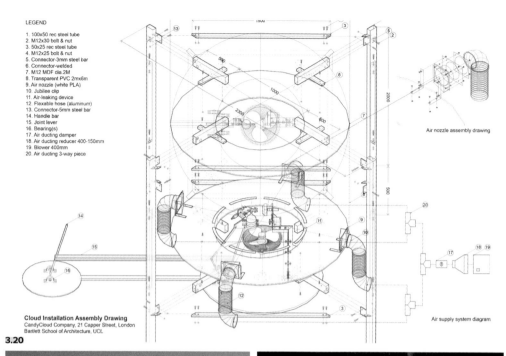

LEGEND

1. 100x50 rec steel tube
2. M12x30 bolt & nut
3. 50x25 rec steel tube
4. M12x25 bolt & nut
5. Connector-3mm steel bar
6. Connector-welded
7. M12 MDF dia 2M
8. Transparent PVC 2mx6m
9. Air nozzle (white PLA)
10. Jubilee clip
11. Air-leaking device
12. Flexable hose (aluminum)
13. Connector-5mm steel bar
14. Handle bar
15. Joint lever
16. Bearing(s)
17. Air ducting damper
18. Air ducting reducer 400-150mm
19. Blower 400mm
20. Air ducting 3-way piece

Air nozzle assembly drawing

Cloud Installation Assembly Drawing
CandyCloud Company, 21 Capper Street, London
Bartlett School of Architecture, UCL

Air supply system diagram

3.20

3.21

3.22

3.20 Shichong Li Cloud Sculptor. Exploded axonometric drawing of the Candy Cloud Cyclone Chamber. Drawing describes how air, sugar supply and temperature are controlled. **3.21** Environmental experiment produced in Arctic Circle Expedition by RC3 Studio. Experiment observed changes in molten sugar fibre extrusion as the bitterly cold temperatures dropped to -25 °C. **3.22 Shichong Li** Cloud Sculptor. Excerpt from photo studies of sugar formation. **3.23 Chryssa Varna, Ruairi Glynn** Light Touch. Design and fabrication of the kinetic mechanism of an installation in Buro Happold Office lobby in collaboration with Haptic Architects. The wave fluid motion of the installation was designed as an automaton, cycling the rise and fall of the dramatic natural lighting conditions of the Norwegian landscape - particularly found when low-lying winter sunlight filters through forests. Photograph by Simon Kennedy.

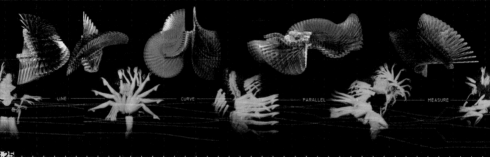

3.24 Chryssa Varna Photo of twin robots with prototype end effectors hung in workshop. Using ideas taken from structured improvisation, a combination of pre-choreographed and improvised performances is designed as a gestural dialogue between a dancer and two robotic performers. The result is an emerging set of movements that conclude to an unpredictable choreography for every performance. **3.25 Chryssa Varna** Notation System. Development of a vocabulary to explain and describe a set of rules based on improvisation techniques. An investigation into whether kinetic design and industrial robotics can embody moving complexity derived from improvisation techniques. **3.26 Chryssa Varna** Render of end effectors. Space and its changes during the choreography have been depicted in the form of two large spatial

modulators. Controllable fans attached to the robots create varying spatial qualities between the dancer and the stage. **3.27 Chryssa Varna** Exploded detailed drawing of the robot arm and end effector. The robot arms have a large range of movement due to a series of 360 rotation joints. The fans have been designed as an opening/closing mechanism which allows a gestural dialog between machine and human. Effectively, the improvisers (i.e. dancer, robots) continuously change their role as being simultaneously their own choreographers and their partners' audience.

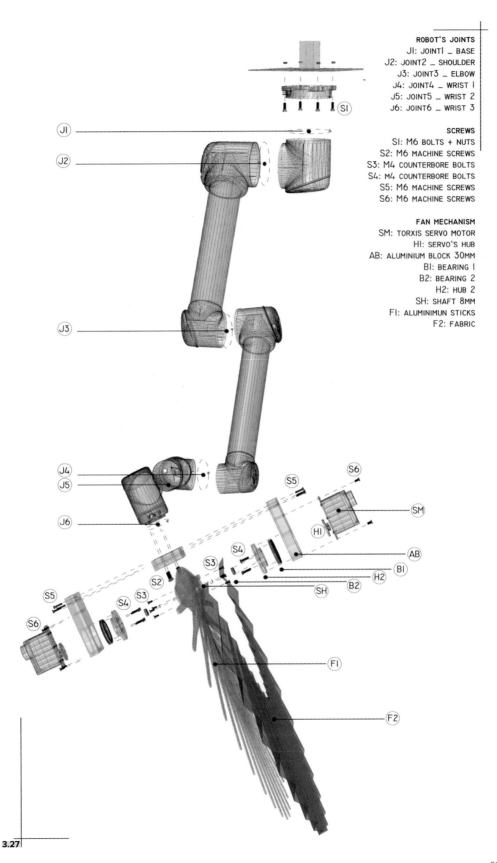

ROBOT'S JOINTS
JI: JOINTI _ BASE
J2: JOINT2 _ SHOULDER
J3: JOINT3 _ ELBOW
J4: JOINT4 _ WRIST 1
J5: JOINT5 _ WRIST 2
J6: JOINT6 _ WRIST 3

SCREWS
SI: M6 BOLTS + NUTS
S2: M6 MACHINE SCREWS
S3: M4 COUNTERBORE BOLTS
S4: M4 COUNTERBORE BOLTS
S5: M6 MACHINE SCREWS
S6: M6 MACHINE SCREWS

FAN MECHANISM
SM: TORXIS SERVO MOTOR
HI: SERVO'S HUB
AB: ALUMINIUM BLOCK 30MM
BI: BEARING 1
B2: BEARING 2
H2: HUB 2
SH: SHAFT 8MM
FI: ALUMINIMUN STICKS
F2: FABRIC

3.27

3.28

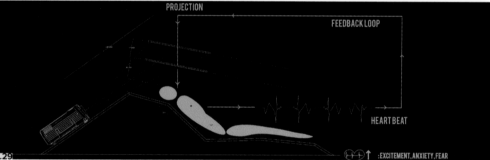

3.29

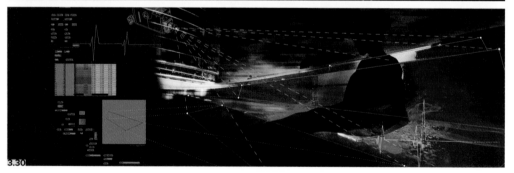

3.30

3.28 – 30 Aimilia Kritikou Pulse Orchestra. An investigation of creating immersive environments through light projection, which alter inhabitant emotional state with continual adaption to occupant behaviour. Heart-rate monitors are embedded within the proposed site – the seatings of The Scoop, an outdoor sunken amphitheatre on the south bank of the River Thames in London. While visitors relax in a reclining position their heart rate measures emotional state and modulates the public space using mapped real-time projections, immersing the visitors, while giving a continuously changing outcome. This investigation proposes a feedback loop between the user's emotional state and the space, through which the space will adapt to the user's emotional changes, and respectively the user will adapt to the visual stimulations of the environment.

3.31 Aimilia Kritikou Modulated Projection. An early prototype creating performative projection of a static frame which embraces and encloses a continual, non-repetitive alternation of patterns. Achieved by encouraging the unpredictable fluid motion of ferrofluid in a gel medium, driven by unsynchronised movements of magnets surrounding it.

3.32

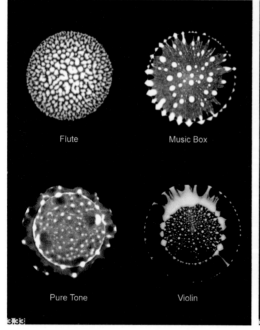

Flute

Music Box

Pure Tone

Violin

3.33

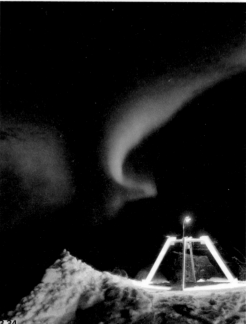

3.34

3.32 Yifan Liu Inspired by the study of Cymatics, an Immersive sound and light installation sited in UCL's North Observatory. Exploring a multisensory architectural performance created through the interaction of sound and material. **3.33 Yifan Liu** Cymatic experiments testing the behaviour of fine silica powder energised by a range of audio inputs. **3.34 Yifan Liu** Sub-zero water based cymatics tests produced in Arctic Circle Expedition by RC3 Studio. Experiments attempted to observe change in Cymatic behaviour as the temperature dropped to -25°C. In the background, the northern lights perform their own mesmerising patterns. The site also inspired Yifan to design her final project in the astrological setting of UCL's Observatory. **3.35 Yifan Liu** Time-based drawing and photomontage describing the interaction and choreography of penultimate sound installation. It shows how the hanging instrument responds to human behaviour in digital and analogue mediums simultaneously.

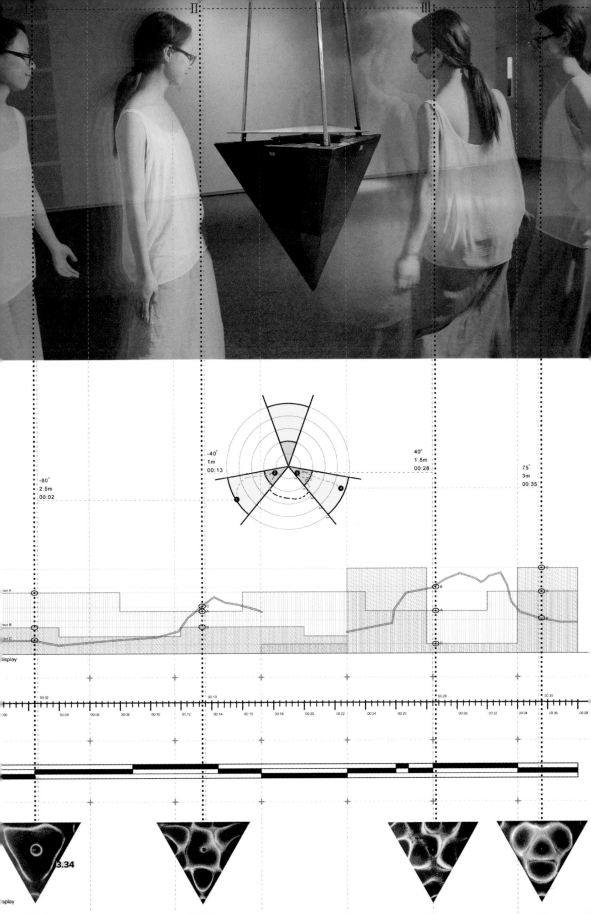

Research
Cluster

Digital Works

Xavier De Kestelier

Computational design and digital fabrication are central to the research agenda of Research Cluster 4 (RC4). Both can be seen as architectural methodologies, the first is often perceived as a pure design methodology while the latter implies a particular method of making. Both methods can often operate individually, but we would argue that this limits its true potential. It is by hybridising computational design and digital fabrication that we can break free of previous connotations of the digital and fully exploit computational design potential. We are interested in a bottom-up approach where computational design and digital fabrication are both the driver and the driven, where both are interested in the digital and material processes to achieve fitness. The designer therefore becomes a listener to the behaviours in this process, and acts as one of many forces in the evolution of its design evolution.

To test this hypothesis RC4 started this year with the 3D-printed bike project. Each group of students was given a particular part of a bike: saddle, tyre, handlebars, etc. Each of these was analysed as an assembly of parts, with each part having its own particular materiality and function. These assemblies were then redesigned with 3D printing as a manufacturing technique. Although this limits the design to only one material, the geometrical freedom becomes limitless. The classical design paradigm of parts and assembly needs to be completely rethought, to open up new design strategies. A good example of this was the redesign of the handlebars with integrated functionality by Jada and Annie. Agnete and Richard applied structural optimisation and microstructures into the design of their saddle and Anton and Zahra developed a saddle that actively adapts and supports the leg movements of the cyclist. The rubber inner and outer tires were replaced by a flexible airless system by ZZ and Fangli. Each of the designs was tested through digital and physical systems and the end result was a prototype of a functional bicycle that could be tested on the road.

Computational design delivers the potential to handle large and complex sets of data, in real-time from remote locations which would otherwise be impossible to coordinate and manipulate manually or in an iterative manner. This allows us to quantify large sets of parameters from spatial to engineering aspects of design through virtual simulations. It is during simulation that we are able to evolve material and fabrications systems for conditions beyond what can be found in the natural situations. These systems can be diverse but extremely precise by continuously being optimised through their response to their host environment. Optimisation as a term is often seen as a part of an engineering discourse, but through computation has found its way into the architectural design discourse.

Each of the RC4 students researched one particular architectural aspect that was then tested, analysed and optimised on both a digital and physical level. One group of students was inspired by adaptive structural systems. ZZ and Fangli took the scissor system often found in the work of Chuck Hoberman and developed it further and added a second level of adaptability. Both Zahra and Jada designed modular systems that adapt to their environment and influence the spatial performance. The first one is a shading device that changes its geometry according to the solar radiation received by the building. The second is an acoustic system that can change its performance from being a sound deflector to a sound absorber.

Throughout the year, RC4 was exposed to various digital fabrication technologies and how they are applied in large projects on site. Therefore we visited various sites, from small-scale projects such as the Kreod pavilion and the FACIT villa all the way to the Louis Vuitton Foundation, which is one of the most exuberantly digitally fabricated buildings. Adaptation and change over time was investigated by both Agnete and Richard. Inspired by the work of the Long Now Foundation, Agnete developed a self-generating structure that erects itself over a period of hundreds of years and is triggered by rising sea levels.

Richard experimented with quantum levitation and after building his own levitating superconductor track he developed a business district that spatially fluctuates according to constant changing markets. Both Annie and Anton developed new construction methods. Annie had a fascination with high performance fabric constructions found in sportswear and spacesuits. She designed a new structural skin based on reciprocal and air beam systems. Anton combined both traditional wood construction with CNC technology to design an outpost for the extreme weather conditions found in northern Siberia.

RC4's Technical Tutors this year were Josef Musil (Grasshopper, Millipede), Arthur Van Der Harten (Pachyderm) and Daniel Piker (Kangeroo). Our Report Tutor was Bruce Davison, ALA.

We are grateful to our critics: Suzy Antinow, Daniel Bosia, Bruce Davison, Jethro Hon, Alvin Huang, Sam Joyce, Dirk Krolikowski, Josef Musil, Michael Pelken, Caroline Reid, Ivan Del Renzio, Jenny Sabin, Rob Slater, Tijl Vanmeirhaeghe, Hugh Whitehead. We thank our sponsors EOS and partners Smartgeometry.

Students
Jada Abubakar, Anton Boganskyi, Renyuan (Richard) Cui, Zahra Ghorbani, Agnete Jukneviciute, Eun Hee (Annie) Kim, Fangli Liu, Zi Zeng

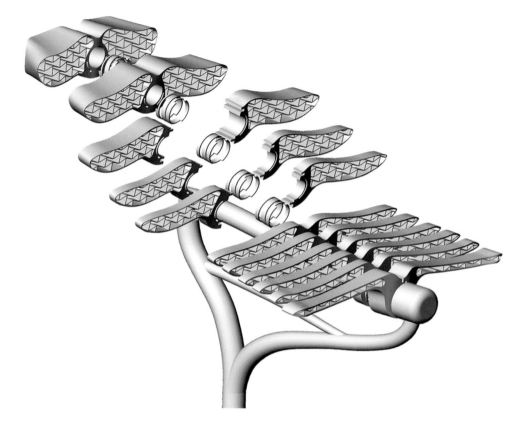

4.1

4.2

4.1 Anton Boganskyi, Zahra Ghorbani 3D-printed Bike Saddle. Digital model that shows the assembly of a new concept for a bike saddle, which actively adapts and supports the leg movement of the cyclist. **4.2 Renyuan Cui, Agnete Jukneviciute** 3D-printed Bike Saddle. The geometry of the bike saddle has been analysed through structural topological optimisation software. A variety of load cases were analysed which then informed the final design of the saddle post.

4.3

4.3 RC4 3D-printed Bike. Each student selected a component of the bicycle which was then redesigned with additive manufacturing technology in mind.

4.4

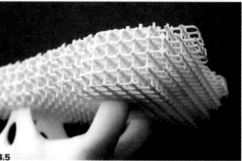

4.5

4.6

4.7

4.4 All bike components were manufactured with high-end 3D printing technology at The Bartlett's Digital Manufacturing Centre with sponsorship of EOS. **4.5 Renyuan Cui, Agnete Jukneviciute** 3D-printed Bike Saddle. The saddle is topologically optimised for both structure and comfort. The differentiating microstructure could only be manufactured with 3D printing technology. **4.6 Jada Abubakar, Eun Hee Kim** 3D-printed Handlebars. The handlebars have integrated brakes and lighting. Each handlebar can also be customised for the preferred hand positions of the cyclist. **4.7 Anton Boganskyi, Zahra Ghorbani** 3D-printed Bike Saddle. The 3D-printed bike saddle can continuously adapt itself to the position of the cyclist. **4.8 Zi Zeng, Fangli Liu** 3D-printed bike wheel. ZZ and Fangli proudly show off their airless tire. The tire has been geometrically optimised for both strength and flexibility. The final design would have been almost impossible to build without 3D printing technology.

4.8

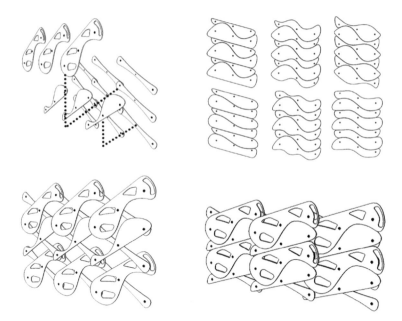

4.9

4.10

4.9 – 4.10 Renyuan Cui, Zahra Ghorbani Adaptable Louvre System. In the first few weeks of RC4, the students were asked to design and manufacture an adaptable system for the building in which the RC4 studio is located: the Royal Ear Hospital. Richard and Zahra designed an adaptable louvre system for the east and west facade of the studio. **4.10** All digital investigations have to be checked on a physical level. Although Ecotect was used to check the performance of the louvre, a physical mock-up was made to verify these findings.

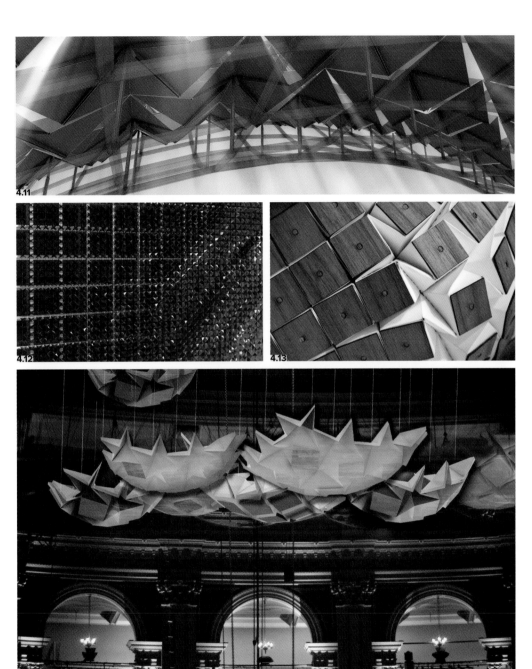

4.11 – 4.12 Zahra Ghorbani Adaptable Façade. Working further on the earlier louvre systems, Zahra investigated the use of passive adaptable shading systems. These systems work on both a technical and cultural level within an arabic context. **4.12** The adaptable system is activated by sunlight and heath through an integrated shape memory alloy component. **4.13 – 4.14 Jada Abubakar** Acoustical Activators. **4.13** Physical model of acoustic panel that can change its perfomance from acoustic deflection to absorbtion. **4.14** Rendering of the acoustical activators in the Royal Albert Hall. The perfomance of the activators was tested out physically and digitally through an acoustical simulation software (Pachyderm).

4.15

4.16

4.17

4.18

4.15 – 4.19 Agnete Jukneviciute Long Now. The Long Now project was inspired by the Long Now Foundation and investigates architecture that erects itself over hundreds of years. **4.15** This rendering shows a half erected project triggered by rising sea levels. **4.16** Several algorithms were developed to investigate the unfolding of geometric shapes. **4.17** Rendering showing a half-erected structure triggered by rising sea levels. **4.18** Physical model showing the self-erection of the structure. For this physical test, melting ice was used as an activator. **4.19** Rendering of a self-erecting structure triggered by rising sea levels.

The Bartlett School of Architecture 2013

4.19

4.20

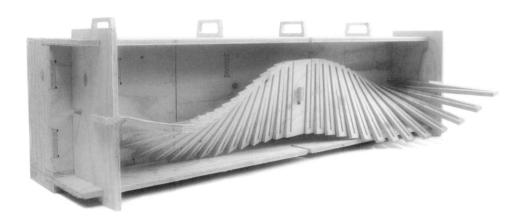

4.21

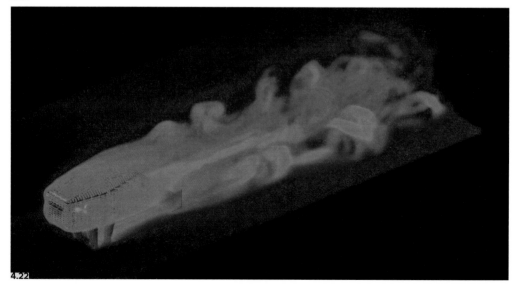

4.22

4.23

4.20– 4.23 Anton Boganskyi Siberian Outpost. **4.20** Physical
model of an onsite CNC-cut residential module for a Siberian
outpost. **4.21** Physical mock-up of a wall element with
integrated snowcatcher. All of the parts are CNC-cut
and assembled with a snap fit connection. The module
collects snow which then functions as a thermal insulator.
4.22 Digital wind simulation of an outpost module. The
roughness of the façade makes the module ideal for catching
snow. **4.23** Digital rendering of how an outpost can grow to a
more substantial network in the northern regions of Siberia.

4.24

4.25

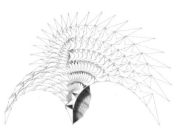

4.24 – 4.26 Zi Zeng, Fangli Liu Walker 4.24 Rendering
of adaptable scissor structure within an urban context.
4.25 Computational diagrams of the adaptable scissor
structures. The basis for this research was the adaptable
structures of Chuck Hoberman. **4.26** The research for this
project was executed through both computational and
physical models.

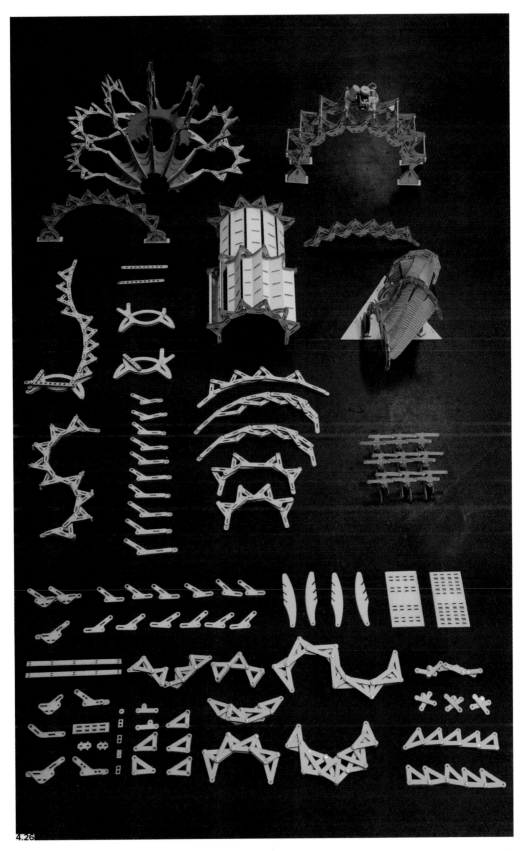

4.26

4.27

4.28

4.27 – 4.29 Renyuan Cui Quantum Levitation. **4.27** Quantum levitation experiment, where a superconductor is cooled within liquid nitrogen and placed on top of a magnetic rail. **4.28** Rendering of a proposal for a business district built from modular blocks that can be continuously reconfigured through quantum levitation. **4.29** Detailed rendering of business district, with components that are being reconfigured according to continuously evolving markets.

4.30

4.30 – 4.31 Eun Hee Kim Reciprocal Airbeams. **4.30** Mock-up of integrated structural skin that combines the concepts of reciprocal structures with tensairity airbeams. **4.31** The integrated reciprocal airbeams were extensively tested trough physical models and are based on a double-layered skin, similar to the construction of kite surfing kites.

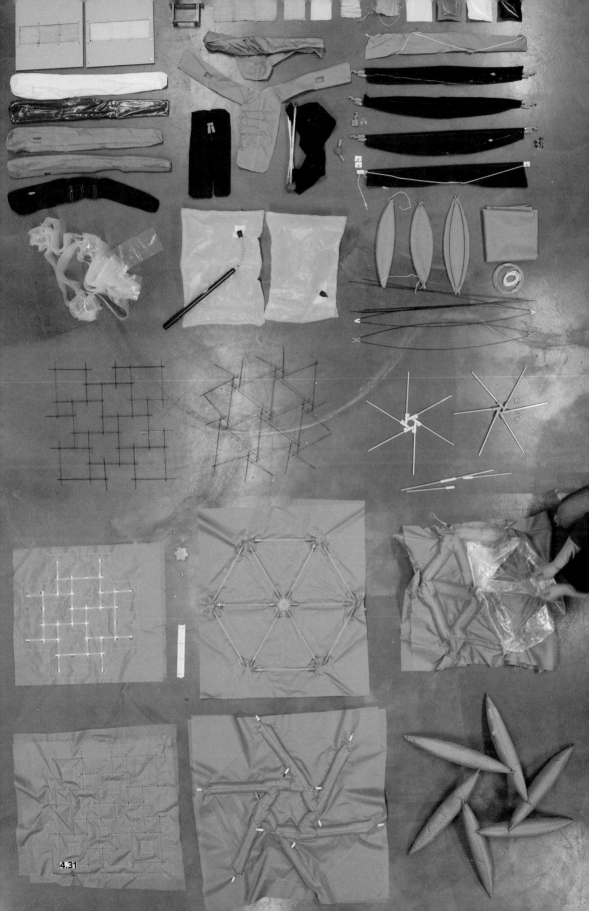

4.31

Research
Cluster

Applications of Robotics to Discrete and Continuous Spatial Lattices

Philippe Morel, Thibault Schwartz

The Bartlett School of Architecture 2013

The past ten years of architectural research, more intimately related to algorithmic and other computational methodologies, have highlighted a massive use of discrete mathematical models. Whether through cellular automata and (multi) agent-based modelling, or due to the intrinsic discrete nature of modern computational processes, the way in which we deal with mathematics has radically evolved. This evolution has not been fully addressed within the discipline of architecture, which remains largely influenced by continuous models of geometrical thinking. Beyond the fact that architecture is usually highly hybridised and component-based – and therefore discrete – our use of continuous models persists because of the phenomenology of our perception or due to diverse constructive traditions. Even if contemporary approaches inspired by rapid prototyping techniques allow us to envision a more perfect continuous future, it seems that, in architecture, discrete and continuous logics are still highly intricate, due to diverse practical constraints that include transportability or a machine's maximum fabrication size. Therefore, either because of the embedded complexity of architecture which differs from sculpture, because of idiosyncratic constructive practices, because of the multiple disciplinary uses of mathematical models, or simply because of the diverse intrinsic logics of materials, the discrete vs. continuous problem cannot be escaped. All this is especially true when one tries to associate highly different logics such as the discrete logic of Cellular Automata in computer simulations and the usually continuous logic of concrete in construction.

This confrontation between contradictory logics lies at the heart of the Research Cluster 5's (RC5) application of robotics to discrete and continuous spatial lattices. By following Henri Poincaré's conventionalist viewpoint in his philosophy of mathematics, asserting that 'one geometry cannot be truer than another, it can merely be more convenient',[1] we challenge the architectural and constructive relevance of novel branches of

geometry including Digital Geometry. First created in order to overcome the limits of 'the usual notions of Cartesian geometries and also the notions of approximate mathematical analysis'[2] in the domain of image analysis, this branch is gaining importance, due partly to the rapidly evolving amount of images available through the Internet. In more and more fields associated with materiality – e.g. in medical imaging where for instance a body organ has to be precisely modelled – the adequacy between the reality of the geometric object studied and its digital model is a crucial issue. In order to attain such accuracy, every source of error or approximation has to be minimised or removed. This is the case with real numbers that necessitate floating point arithmetic in order to be correctly represented in a computer, and is one of the reasons why Digital Geometry only deals with integers. According to Jean Françon, in Digital Geometry an object 'is considered as a geometrical object in a discrete space (a set of points with whole coordinates). Digital geometry studies geometry in such a space without reference to the usual Cartesian geometry. The continuous is abandoned, a very radical position. The only links between digital geometry and Cartesian geometry are in the analogy of notions and the geometer's inspiration for these analogies [...] it then appears that a notion of the continuous naturally produces several non-equivalent discrete definitions by analogy.'[3]

Even if we are not entirely convinced that 'the discrete theory will reach the point where we jettison the idea that the discrete is an approximation of the continuous'[4] and that 'one day we will think and calculate in a single geometry, which will be totally discrete and totally adapted to discrete machines',[5] we have to admit that the exponentially growing refinement of discretisation is producing a new and strong contemporary phenomenology. Beyond the speculative aspect of such a phenomenology, which is 'subversive because it contests the absolute reign of the continuous in geometry',[6] RC5 emphasises its

The Bartlett School of Architecture 2013

practical consequences. The most interesting one is related to the performances of recent fibre-reinforced materials such as carbon tubes or plates and high-performance concretes. Thanks to their lightness, fluidity or ductility, such materials allow us to deal with the fine grain of computer simulations. Contrary to the modernist optimal structures mostly derived from two dimensional surfaces, quasi-optimal computational architecture structures are based on large data sets that give rise to larger topological and geometrical configurations. While most of these configurations can be represented through analytic representations thanks to the flexibility of contemporary parametric functions, it can be highly inefficient to follow such a path, particularly when architectural geometries based on Agent or CA processes are natively expressed by a couple of simple rules.

According to these elements, through the use of Mathematica, Grasshopper and the HAL robot control plugin for Grasshopper, this year RC5 investigated novel applications of robotics to constructions and challenge our perception of architecture. In addition to the studio work and to the regular classes on Grasshopper and HAL with Thibault Schwartz, the Cluster organised two open robotic workshops (based on the new ABB IRB120 robot), one workshop with guest engineers and architects Lucia Mondardini and Martina Presepi dedicated to the realisation of a nexorade-based dome made of robotically cut foam ashlars, and five lectures given by computer and material scientists, engineers and architects: Niccolo Baldassini, Nicolas Bredeche, Justin Dirrenberger, Lucia Mondardini and Andrew Witt.

We are grateful to our sponsors, Voxeljet.

Students

Min Su Kim, Sangyoon Kim, Yoojin Kim, Xiaohui (Sophia) Liu, Jung Woong (PJ) Park, Di Peng, Yiqiao (Erica) Wang, Yuzhe Wang, Zhouhui Wang, Shi Yin, Xuejing (Ellie) Yu, Chao (Richard) Yue

1. H. Poincaré, 'Non-Euclidean Geometries' in *Science and Hypothesis*, 1905
2. Jean Françon, foreword to *Géométrie Discrète et Images Numériques*, Editions Lavoisier, Paris, 2007
3. Ibid.
4. Jean Françon, Ibid. The main proponents of American Digital Philosophy share the same view, enriched with specific philosophical hypotheses
5. Jean Françon, Ibid.
6. Ibid.

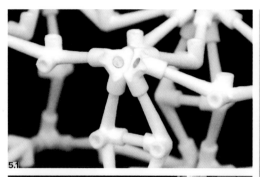

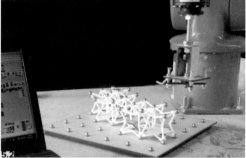

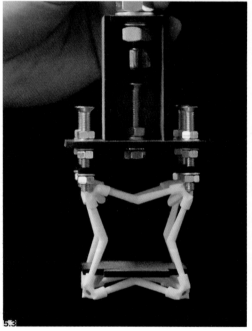

5.1 – 5.8 Chao Yue Modular Design in Polyominoes & Polycubes. **5.1** Detail of a rapid-prototyped constructive module with embedded magnets at each corner (corresponding to vertices in a more abstract representation based on graphs). The standard magnets are to be replaced in the 1:1 scale model by electro-permanent ones. This project is based on the possibilities offered by polyominoes for the approximation of various unregular shapes, as well as for the generation of complex spatial trajectories which can be robotically produced, thanks to their discrete nature. **5.2** Assembling of the modules on an elementary cartesian grid. The robot used is an ABB IRB 120, while the trajectories (in Rapid code) are computed with HAL. **5.3** The permanent magnets are associated in such a way that they replicate

differences of power otherwise coming from electromagnets. Therefore no programming is necessary here to simulate the discrete events: they occur 'naturally', as with regular magnet systems and toys. **5.4** A robotically assembled model of a building. The various trajectories result from combinations of polycubes approximating continuous paths. The reachability of each module is computed beforehand in order to establish an assembly plan (avoiding bumps and conflicting positions), but they could also be computed dynamically and hence could make use of the streaming capabilities of HAL.

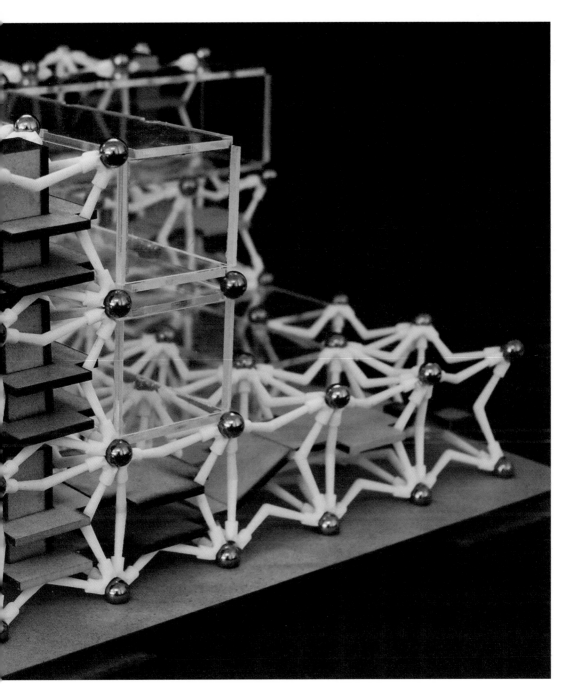

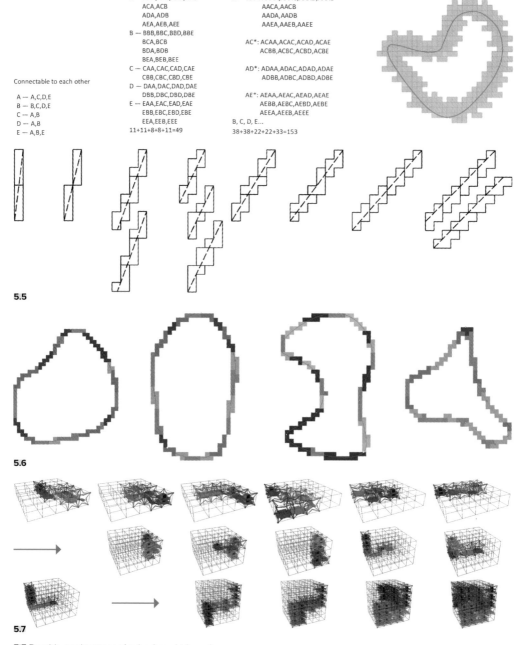

Tricubes

A — AAA,AAC,AAD,AAE
ACA,ACB
ADA,ADB
AEA,AEB,AEE
B — BBB,BBC,BBD,BBE
BCA,BCB
BDA,BDB
BEA,BEB,BEE
C — CAA,CAC,CAD,CAE
CBB,CBC,CBD,CBE
D — DAA,DAC,DAD,DAE
DBB,DBC,DBD,DBE
E — EAA,EAC,EAD,EAE
EBB,EBC,EBD,EBE
EEA,EEB,EEE
11+11+8+8+11=49

Tetracubes

A — AA*: AAAA,AAAC,AAAD,AAAE
AACA,AACB
AADA,AADB
AAEA,AAEB,AAEE

AC*: ACAA,ACAC,ACAD,ACAE
ACBB,ACBC,ACBD,ACBE

AD*: ADAA,ADAC,ADAD,ADAE
ADBB,ADBC,ADBD,ADBE

AE*: AEAA,AEAC,AEAD,AEAE
AEBB,AEBC,AEBD,AEBE
AEEA,AEEB,AEEE

B, C, D, E...
38+38+22+22+33=153

Connectable to each other

A — A,C,D,E
B — B,C,D,E
C — A,B
D — A,B
E — A,B,E

5.5

5.6

5.7

5.5 Possible combinations of polycubes which can be assembled together in sequence. On the right the spline curve shows how a thick line made of polyominoes (here in 2D) can approximate a continuous trajectory, and (below) how these polyominoes can adapt to different slopes. **5.6** Approximation of different curves (and curvature) with a series of polyominoes, here in 2D. **5.7** Spatial scenarii in a one layer (equivalent to a 2D) map, 3 layers and 5 layers. The design of the discrete path is generative while based on approximations of continuous pre-existing lines and surfaces. **5.8** A piece of the approx. 400 line script describing the rules to be followed by the polycubes.

```
'==========================================================
'Bottom Detail Conditions
'==========================================================

Public Sub Bottom (ByVal PrevFam As Integer, ByVal Seed As Integer, ByVal PrevPt As
Point3d, ByVal CurrPt As Point3d, ByVal NextPt As Point3d, ByRef Family As Integer)
    If PrevFam = 1 And Seed = 0 Then Family = 1
    If PrevFam = 1 And Seed = 1 Or Seed = 2 Then
        If NextPt.X - CurrPt.X = 0 And NextPt.Z - CurrPt.Z <> 0 Then Family = 7
        If NextPt.X - CurrPt.X > 0 Then Family = 17
        If NextPt.X - CurrPt.X < 0 Then Family = 13
    End If

    If PrevFam = 2 Then
        If NextPt.X - CurrPt.X = 0 And Seed = 0 Then Family = 2
        If NextPt.X - CurrPt.X = 0 And Seed = 1 Or Seed = 2 Then Family = 5
        If NextPt.X - CurrPt.X < 0 Then Family = 18
        If NextPt.X - CurrPt.X > 0 Then Family = 12
    End If

    If PrevPt.z - CurrPt.z <> 0 Then Family = 11
    If PrevPt.z - CurrPt.z = 0 Then
        If (PrevFam = 3 Or PrevFam = 5 Or PrevFam = 6) And (Seed = 0 Or Seed = 1) Then
Family = 1
        If PrevFam = 7 And (Seed = 0 Or Seed = 1) Then Family = 2
        If (PrevFam = 3 Or PrevFam = 5 Or PrevFam = 6 Or PrevFam = 7) And Seed = 2 Then
Family = 11
        If PrevFam = 14 Or PrevFam = 16 Then Family = 2
        If PrevFam = 15 Or PrevFam = 19 Then Family = 1
        If PrevFam = 11 And Seed = 0 Then Family = 1
        If PrevFam = 11 And Seed = 1 Then Family = 1
        If PrevFam = 11 And Seed = 2 Then Family = 2
    End If
End Sub

'==========================================================
'Top Detail Conditions
'==========================================================

Public Sub Top (ByVal PrevFam As Integer, ByVal Seed As Integer, ByVal PrevPt As Point3d,
ByVal CurrPt As Point3d, ByVal NextPt As Point3d, ByRef Family As Integer)
    If PrevFam = 1 And Seed = 0 Then Family = 1
    If PrevFam = 1 And Seed = 1 Or Seed = 2 Then
        If NextPt.X - CurrPt.X = 0 And NextPt.Z - CurrPt.Z <> 0 Then Family = 5
        If NextPt.X - CurrPt.X > 0 Then Family = 15
        If NextPt.X - CurrPt.X < 0 Then Family = 19
    End If

    If PrevFam = 2 Then
        If NextPt.X - CurrPt.X = 0 And Seed = 0 Then Family = 2
        If NextPt.X - CurrPt.X = 0 And Seed = 1 Or Seed = 2 Then Family = 7
        If NextPt.X - CurrPt.X < 0 Then Family = 14
        If NextPt.X - CurrPt.X > 0 Then Family = 16
    End If
```

5.8

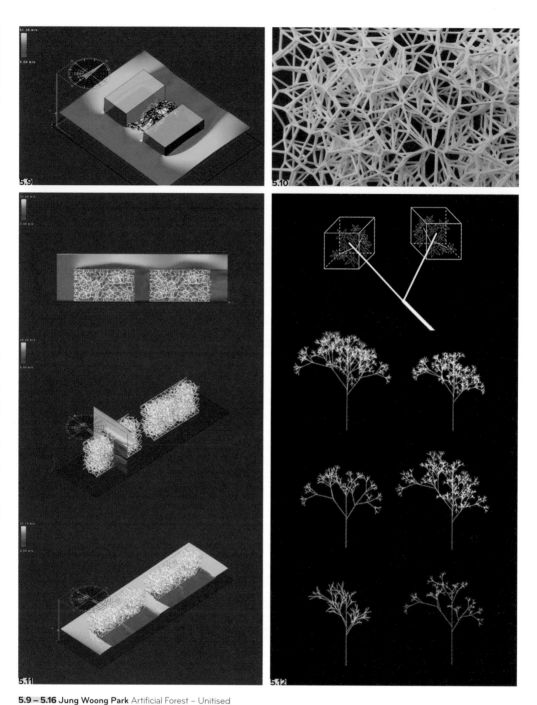

5.9 – 5.16 Jung Woong Park Artificial Forest – Unitised Canopy. The project investigates the power offered by spatial setups based on computer simulations of canopies to create performative physical models. These models provide sun and wind protections, as well as protection against the rain. When carefully looking at a canopy, one discovers a complex intricacy of natural layers giving birth to a proper ecosystem. For the aforementioned performances, the tree species is the most important parameter (the size of the tree, its branching system, its leaves, etc.). **5.10** Rapid-prototyped model of a simulated canopy (whose shape of course does not mimic the original). **5.12** Computer simulation of different species of tree.

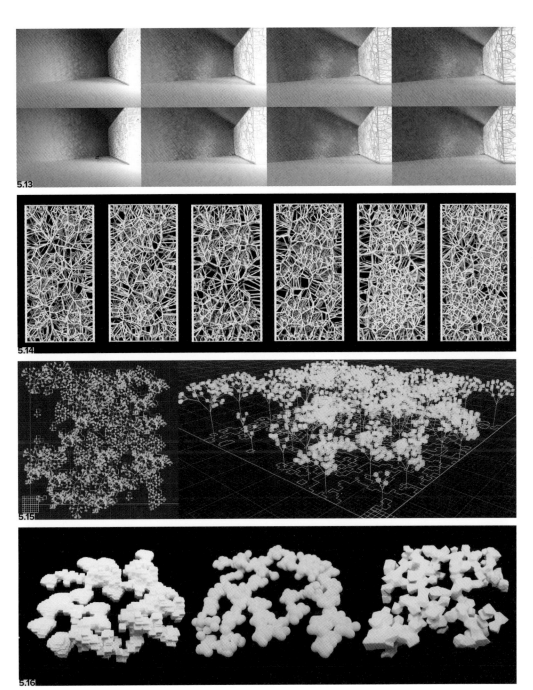

5.13 Lighting simulations with different densities of canopy-based thick panels ('canopy blocks'). **5.14** Blocks with different shapes but similar properties. **5.15** GA-based growth of a canopy with corresponding shadowing density. **5.16** Representation of groups of leaves: cube, sphere, voronoi cells. These models are used as representations rather than as formal models. The facility which is offered by the voronoi representation for partitioning (and packing) the space allows for an easier correspondence between the stochastic model (present in the genetic algorithm) and the entirely deterministic model necessary for the 1:1 scale fabrication.

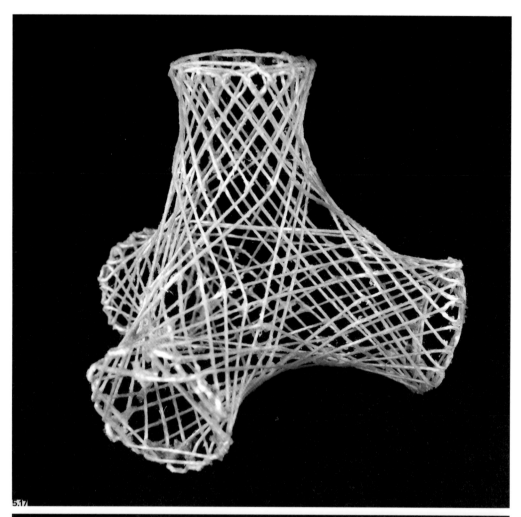

5.17

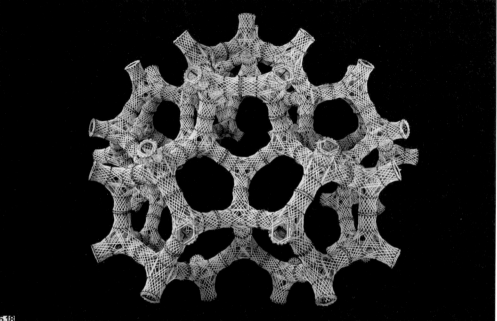

5.18

5.17 – 5.18 Shi Yin and Zhouhui Wang Modular Weaving System Generation Aided by 6-Axis Industrial Robot. The project is based on the assembly of robotically woven 4 (or more) branche modules. Robot trajectories are computed with HAL on the fly, whatever the weaving paths. **5.19 – 5.23 Xiaohui Liu** Structure with Interlocking Joint and Robotic Application. The project, first based on traditional Japanese wood joints, establishes its own original interlocking system inspired by interlocking puzzles, in order to allow for a robotic assembling (the order of operations is much simplified). Wooden pieces are CNC milled on 3-axis machines.

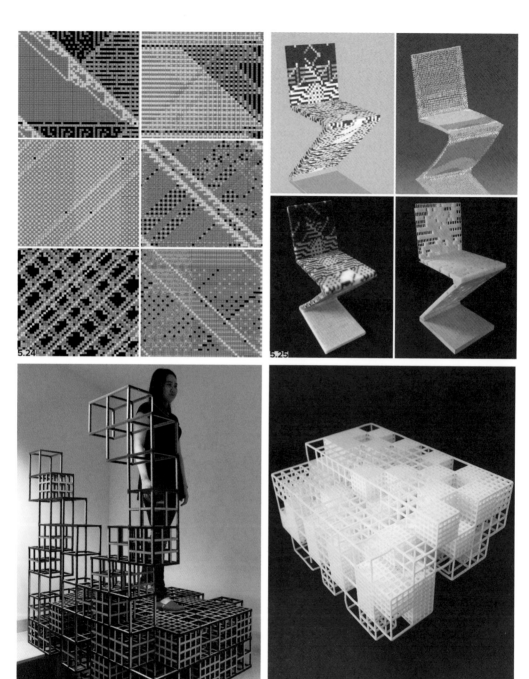

5.24 – 5.28 Minsu Kim CA: Understanding of the Animal
Pattern Formation System through Cellular Automata and
the Adaptation of Architectural Design. Project based on a
precise control of CA behaviours (crossing deterministic and
non-deterministic approaches, allowing the generation of
architectural structures with various mechanical and spatial
properties). Automata cells are physically 'translated' into
cubic cells of varying strength solid materials, then into various
density hollow structures made of wooden pieces (for which
the joints are given by Xiaohui Liu). **5.25** First application on a
canonical Z chair model. **5.26** Larger scale application: a piece
of a bridge structure. **5.27** Rapid prototyped model showing
the density of voids. **5.28** 3D-printed model of a bridge
structure made of varying strength continuous material.

5.28

Geometry of Degree - 4 Flat foldable Vertex.

$$f : \cos P_{BC} \rightarrow \cos P_{AB}$$
$$f^{-1} : \cos P_{AB} \rightarrow \cos P_{BC}$$
$$\cos P_{BC} = f^{-1}(\cos P_{AB}) = -k + \frac{1-k^2}{\cos P_{AB} - k}$$

< Basic Constraints >
1. $(0 < \theta_A < \pi, \; 0 < \theta_D < \pi, \; \pi \le \theta_A + \theta_D)$
2. $\theta_C = \pi - \theta_A$ and $\theta_D = \pi - \theta_B$
3. $P_{CD} = -P_{AB}$ and $P_{DA} = P_{BC}$

$$P_{BC} = Arccos\left(-k + \frac{1-k^2}{\cos P_{AB} - k}\right)$$

Geometry to Hull

$$\cos(\pi - P_{AB}) = \cos(\pi - P_{BC}) - \frac{\sin^2(\pi - P_{BC})\sin\theta_A \sin\theta_D}{1 - \cos E}$$

$$\cos E = -\cos\theta_A \cos\theta_B + \sin\theta_A \sin\theta_B \cos(\pi - P_{BC})$$

E = angle between l_{AD} and l_{CD}

$$f : \cos P_{BC} \rightarrow \cos P_{AB} :$$
$$\cos P_{AB} = f(\cos P_{BC}) = k + \frac{1-k^2}{\cos P_{BC} + k}$$
$$\left(k \cdot k(\theta_A, \theta_D) = \frac{1 + \cos\theta_A \cos\theta_D}{\sin\theta_A \sin\theta_D}\right)$$

$$\cos P_{AB} = \left(\frac{1 + \cos\theta_A \cos\theta_B}{\sin\theta_A \sin\theta_D}\right) + \frac{1 - \left(\frac{1+\cos\theta_A \cos\theta_B}{\sin\theta_A \sin\theta_B}\right)^2}{\cos P_{AC} + \left(\frac{1+\cos\theta_A \cos\theta_B}{\sin\theta_A \sin\theta_B}\right)}$$

using basic trigonometric functions like $\cos x = a \rightarrow \cos^{-1} a = x$ or $\cos x = a \rightarrow Arccos a = x$

$$P_{AB} = Arccos\left[\left(\frac{1 + \cos\theta_A \cos\theta_B}{\sin\theta_A \sin\theta_B}\right) + \frac{1 - \left(\frac{1+\cos\theta_A \cos\theta_B}{\sin\theta_A \sin\theta_B}\right)^2}{\cos P_{AC} + \left(\frac{1+\cos\theta_A \cos\theta_B}{\sin\theta_A \sin\theta_B}\right)}\right]$$

Parameters
$\theta_A, \theta_B, Angle(P_{AC}) \rightarrow$ Can translate to "E"

$$= Arccos\left(-\left(\frac{1+\cos\theta_A \cos\theta_B}{\sin\theta_A \sin\theta_D}\right) + \frac{1 - \left(\frac{1+\cos\theta_A \cos\theta_B}{\sin\theta_A \sin\theta_D}\right)^2}{\cos P_{AB} - \left(\frac{1+\cos\theta_A \cos\theta_B}{\sin\theta_A \sin\theta_D}\right)}\right)$$

$$f_{i,j+1}\left(f_{i+1,j+1}^{-1}\left(f_{i+1,j}\left(f_{i,j}^{-1}(x)\right)\right)\right) = I$$

$$f_{i+1,j}\left(f_{i,j}^{-1}(x)\right) = f_{i,j+1}\left(f_{i+1,j+1}^{-1}(x)\right)$$

$$\frac{B_j x + A_j}{A_j x + B_j} = \frac{B_{j+1} x + A_{j+1}}{A_{j+1} x + B_{j+1}} \qquad \langle j' = j, j+1 \rangle$$

$$A_{j'} = -k_{i,j'} + k_{i+1,j'}$$
$$B_{j'} = 1 - k_{i,j'} k_{i+1,j'}$$

$$(A_j B_{j+1} - A_{j+1} B_j)x = (A_j B_{j+1} - A_{j+1} B_j) \equiv 0$$

$$A_j B_{j+1} - A_{j+1} B_j = 0$$

1. developable $\left[2\pi - \sum_{K=1}^{4} \theta_{K,i}\right]_{n \text{ inner vert} \times 1}$
2. Flat foldable $\left[\sum_{K=1}^{4}(-1)^K \theta_{K,i}\right]_{n \text{ inner vert} \times 1} = 0$
3. Planar $\left[p \cdot \text{clause}\right]_{n \text{ panel} \times 1}$

5.29

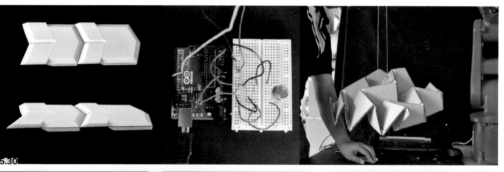

5.30

5.31

5.29 Sangyoon Kim Architectural Design based on Computational Origami. Exploring the realisation of structures and forms exclusively based on rigid origami. In order to implement true rigid origami in the computer (most available plugins for example provide folding algorithms containing deformations, even if small), the underlying trigonometric rules were checked and transformed into algorithms. **5.30** Physical model based on a Miura-Ori crease pattern and activation with an arduino card, and motors. **5.31** Deployment of a larger model, with non deformable fabric as joints. **5.32** Various types of geometry and detail of trigonometric rules.

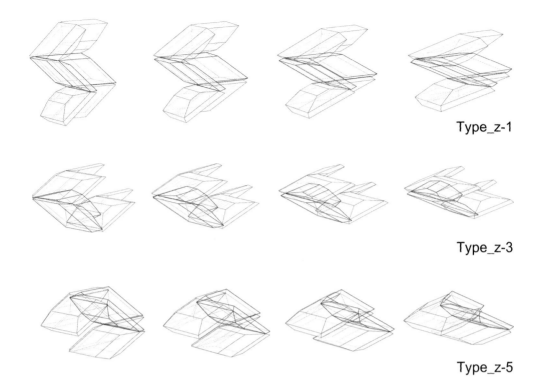

Type_z-1

Type_z-3

Type_z-5

Type_Z-2

Type_Z-4

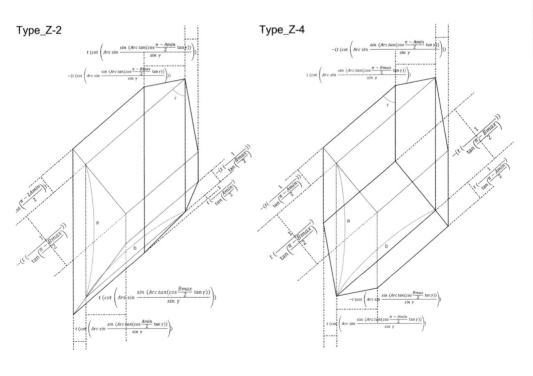

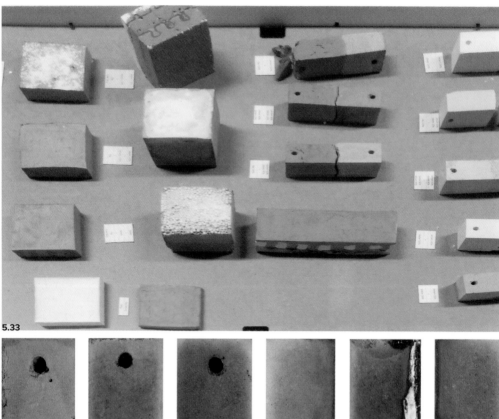

5.33

 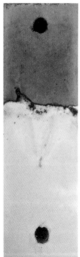    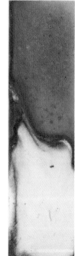

| Strength 31.8N | Strength 35.5N | **Strength 119.2N** | **Strength 136.5N** | **Strength 125.2N** | **Strength 119.2N** |

5.34

5.33 – 5.36 Yoojin Kim Thermo Structure: Chemical Assembly of Materials. Exploring how material can be assembed together without any mechanical fixtures or glue – in fact, without any additional material. It establishes that specific types of clay and specific types of cement can coexist, with interesting mechanical and thermal properties. First, different types of mixtures are tested, addressing their adhesive strength. Then different materials are added, e.g. polystyrene balls, in order to increase the lightness as well as the thermal properties of the compound. Ultimately, the relevance of such a composite 'brick' (which is only one among multiple applications) is proven, as the thermal performances of clay are very high and are a good complement to the poor thermal performances of concrete.

5.35

5.36

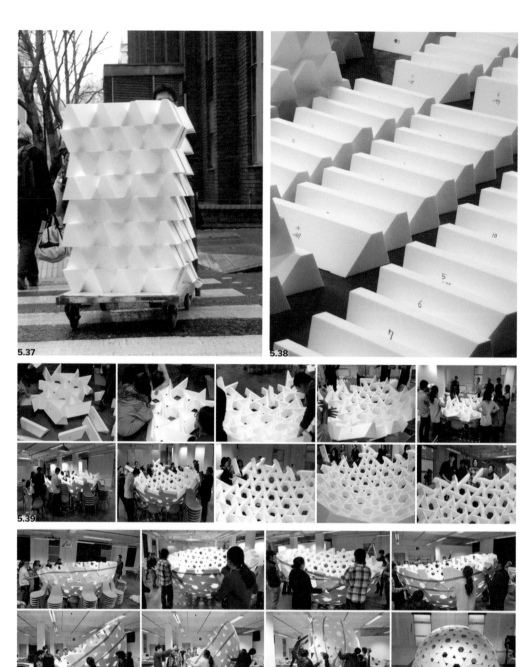

5.37 – 5.41 In March 2013, RC5 organised a five-day workshop with guests engineer and architect-engineer Lucia Mondardini and Martina Presepi, with help from Tristan Gobin. It pursued an earlier induction exercise dedicated to reciprocal structures (nexorades). The workshop was dedicated to the fabrication of a dome, inspired from a model of 'flat vault' conceived by Jospeh Abeille in early 18th Century. 226 robotically cut foam ashlars of 16 different families were finally assembled in a 3m diameter dome. All ashlar geometries were generated in Mathematica®, with varying parameters, based on a .nb file written by Lucia Mondardini. The robot toolpath was automatically generated in HAL. **5.42** A view of the intrados of the final dome.

5.41

5.42

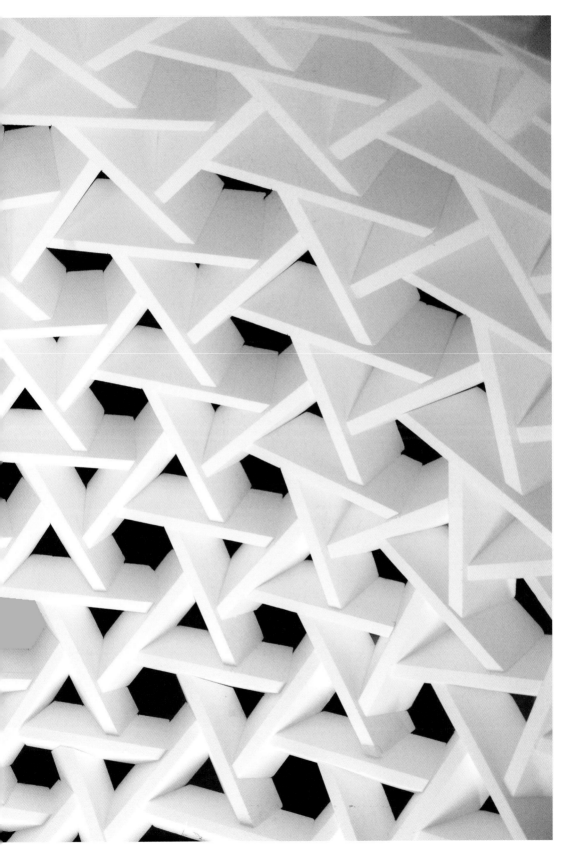

Research
Cluster

DWG Protocols

Luke Pearson

The mediation of space through contemporary technologies of viewing, reading, and occupying is necessarily shifting traditional dialects for mapping and compartmentalising the world around us. These techniques of drawing and charting have often existed for many years, defining boundaries, borders, pressure zones, territories and so forth. Semantically, Green Lines such as those that striate Israel or Nicosia are derived from the act of apportioning swathes of space using a drawn gesture. The thickness of a pen-line on a map may be a point of territorial conjecture, as we see the limitations and obfuscations of a singular drawing tool apportioning spaces at a multitude of scales.

However, new processes of translation, of interpolation through computation are allowing the drawing to renegotiate its position in relation to territories. We may now articulate architectural spaces through appropriated or self-designed tools for the transcription of gesture and movement. Research Cluster 6 works through investigating the delicate interface between new technologies for manifesting architecture physically and the codifications and notations that make up the 'drawing' that guides this materialisation. We are interested in new protocols of translation between gesture, drawing and architecture.

This process may slide back and forth, and apply progressive distortions onto our idea of what it is to delineate space. We clearly need the development of new conventions of drawing to be able to understand this: to allow the architect to reclaim aspects of their field new technology allows them to expropriate and then manifest ways of drawing these new conditions.

Rather than the top-down *kriegspiel* view of the world used to draw up borders on maps, the drawing will become suffuse with the multiple scale shifts, currencies of information and data flows that communicate back and forth with it. However, we still witness slippages, abstractions and inconsistencies in the reading and transcription of places that may prove furtive ground for architectural investigation. For instance the fissure between Google and Apple (TomTom) mapping data that has resulted in roads as mountain ranges, disappearing bridges and vertical rivers. Might we see an equivocal set of landscape phenomena during the early launch of Galileo as a competitor to GPS?

At the same time, we may speculate on how the application of computation and software might be directly related to these territorial slippages or quirks. The cluster examines architectures that may be deployed remotely, assemble with the user in absentia, or resolve phenomena to allow for new ways of seeing. Whether it be geographer Trevor Paglen taking 'limit' photographs of rendition sites in the US using astronomy telephoto lenses, fully automated ports of the world assembling and disassembling giant aggregations of containers, or errors in our GPS resolution caused by our physical position in relation to satellites, we can see how the potential of computation can allow us to reconcile these situations in new ways.

Over the course of the year the students have developed a critical approach towards software, its augmentation and application. They have explored the back and forth translation between the gestural and manufactured, and speculated through demonstrative projects that frame their arguments in the face of sociopolitical catalysts and contexts for projects. Their research engages both with the potential for computation in these processes and how its proliferation into the world-at-large demands our reflection on existing frameworks of understanding and the proposition of new rules of engagement with respect to design and its application. As the capital of finance of the nation at the top of the 'pyramid' of networked society, but a city emblematic of the industrial complex of another era, the Cluster visited New York to investigate potential sites of application that challenge the relationship between drawing and its transmission into built matter.

Students produced individual research projects, which serve as a yearlong process from which they derive architectural outputs and investigations. Each student has driven their own agenda through formulating a critical approach towards drawing, computation and context, building up a series of tactics and design methodologies during Terms 1 and 2, before applying this to architectural design projects through Terms 3 and 4.

The critical responses of the Cluster deal not only with technique, and manifestations of architectures through computational means, but the implication sfor a world where boundaries are increasingly mutable and human protagonists might be increasingly remote from areas with which they engage architecturally. Through speculative manoeuvres into the question of scale and its transferability, students not only test the limits of forms that the drawing may take, but how these may become new drawn conventions for understanding and designing with new types of material, phenomena or ephemera. We have investigated the production and interrogation of new protocols for the production of drawing, and probed the extents of the act to see how it may be reformed anew under the auspice of emerging computational techniques and advanced fabrication.

Thanks to Kristijan Cebzan (Report Supervisor) and Petros Koutsolampros (Technical Advisor).

Students
Ioanna Cheinoporou, Liang Huang, Yi-Chiao (Chiao) Huang, Chia Yi Kuo, Yuchen (Penny) Liu, Chenchao Pan, Yang Yang, Shuyi Zhang

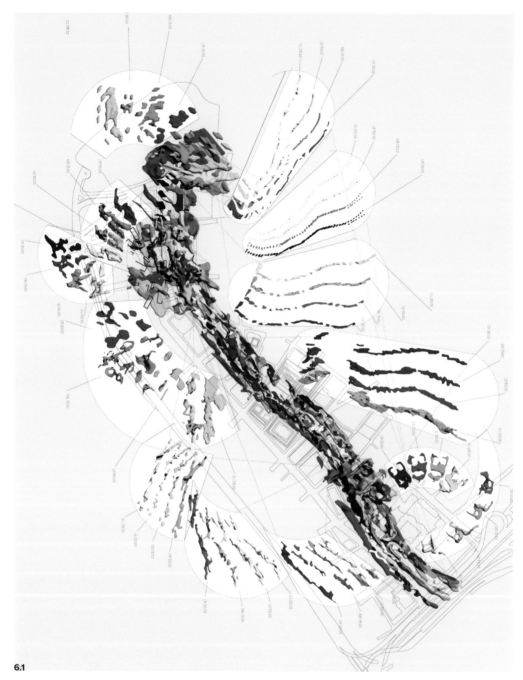

6.1

6.1 – 6.4 Shuyi Zhang Invisible Architectures **6.1** Temporal Territories of Pearl Street. Reviving the history of Pearl Street in Manhattan through an invisible particulate landscape of smells dictated by air flows. This drawing shows the landscapes and spaces generated by the constantly responding system of emitters and sensors that adapt to the prevailing wind condition to maintain a 'cloud' of territories along the streetscape. A series of architectural events of recollection and reorganisation are produced through the interaction of landscapes of smell and the physical infrastructure along the street, that intersect and respond to the shifting air flows within the city. **6.2** Smellscape One. A physical representation of a CFD structure of smell created by a series of emitters and the prevailing wind. Generating architectural forms and spaces through the manipulation of air. **6.3** Smellscape Model. A coloured 3D-printed model of one of the invisible architectural territories showing gradiations of smell strength and encoded with different types and forms. **6.4** Manhattan as Dynamic Landscape of Smells. Using a fluid dynamic system of particles to make a smell map of Manhattan that shows the changing landscapes of air and smell across the city over the course of the year. By defining these parameters for a non-visual landscape of air flow, a series of emitters and elements set up to respond to this would allow for the maintenance of 'still' landscapes through a series of reponses and counterbalances in relation to this ever-shifting meteorological landscape.

6.2

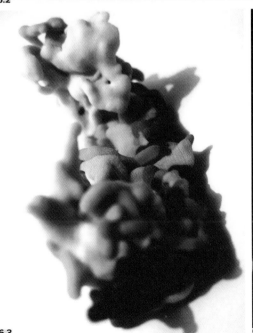

6.3

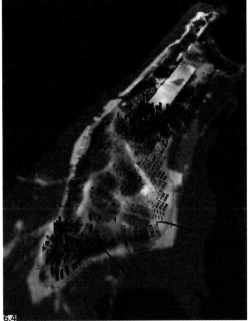

6.4

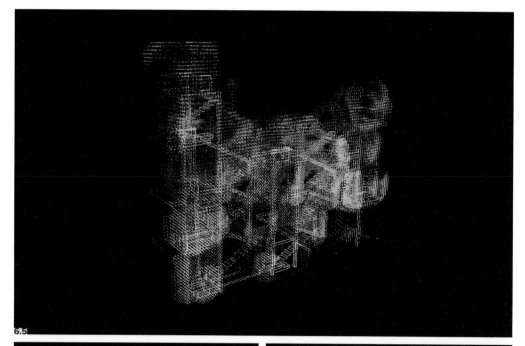

6.5

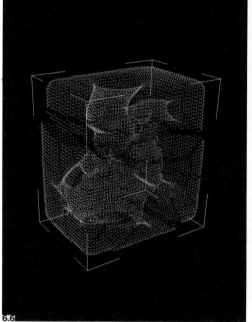

6.6

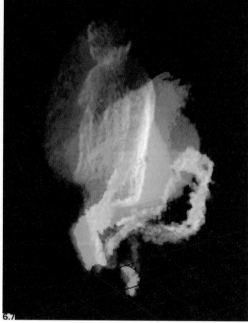

6.7

6.5 – 6.9 Chenchao Pan Rewriting Behavioural Space
6.5 Recording usages and behaviour within a tight city site.
By making a series of recordings using a Kinect, a series of
behavioural patterns are identified, showing the changing
nature and use of space across the day. These recordings
then become a shifting landscape of spaces, a reponsive
architecture that becomes a writing and rewriting of the body
in space. **6.6** Using physical definitions of the body to make
a responsive space. Openings for light and ventilation are
changed in relation to readings of the body in space. A test
into how a landscape of particles is affected and transformed
in its behaviour by the presence of readings and traces of a
body. The colouration shows the velocity of movement of
particles away from the body, as the effect of transforming

space dissapates throughout the structure. **6.7** A reading from
a Kinect sensor of a series of choreographies designed from
everyday behaviour within a typical home. These allow spaces
to be understood as a series of flows and interactions between
people and domestic space. They are then translated into a
series of inferfaces for affecting physical space around bodily
behaviours and movements. **6.8** Drawing examining the
stages of transformation of a space over time, defined by the
occupants' movements carving out traces and turning the
architectural fabric into a series of cave-like structures that
induce new types of inhabitation. **6.9** View cutting through
spaces generated by the movement of inhabitants showing
how they change over time and increase in resolution as
consecutive readings of the body build up within the space.

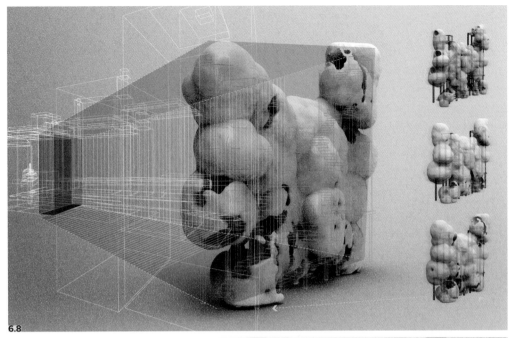

6.8

6.9

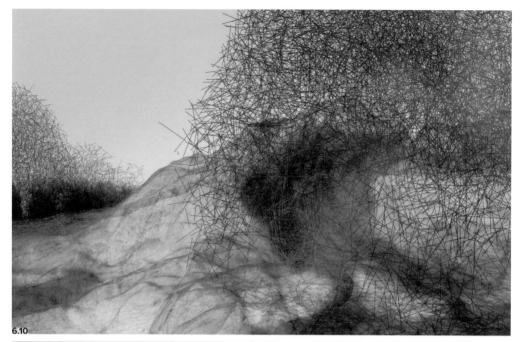

6.10

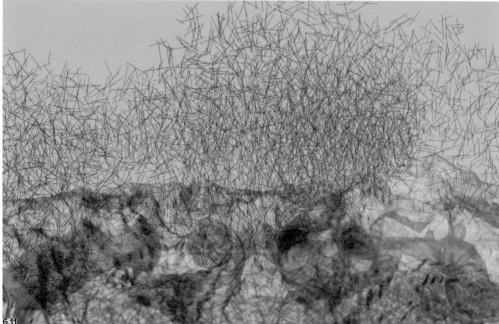

6.11

6.10 – 6.13 Chia Yi Kuo Landscape [re]Interpretation: Atomising Chinese Landscape Painting. Translation is a conversion of presentation to communicate in another language without changing its nature. A further version is generated under observing the primary principles. Fidelity to essence is prior to interpreting literally. In Chinese landscape paintings, spatial perception is beyond the natural experience. It illustrates artistic conception and poetry which is unutterable. Compared to the physical world, artists outline a compelling vision for the ideal landscape to convey the poetics of space and suggest more possibilities. The space in paintings has no definite boundaries, which suggests that extension is infinite. Painters manipulate the two-dimensional syntax to transform and reconstruct three-dimensional elements with certain indispensable principles. During the process of interpretation, the manipulation of brush and ink visualises natural phenomena and constructs depth perception. Based on the principles of Chinese landscape paintings, a methodology is developed to transcribe abstract medium into concrete practice in architectural space and artificial landscapes. It conveys the original poetic conception of space. The retranslation from painting to landscape brings man-made landforms a new definition. Furthermore, an approach derived from representing the textures and patterns of nature can potentially evolve a more compatible typology for physical environments. The translation process investigates a path from 3D-2D-3D. Inspired by the trompe l'oeil rooms many of the great landscape painters built to evoke a more 'authentic'

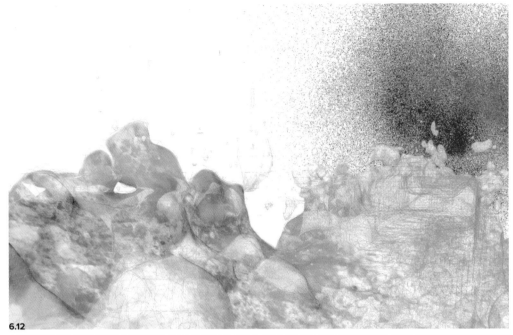

6.12

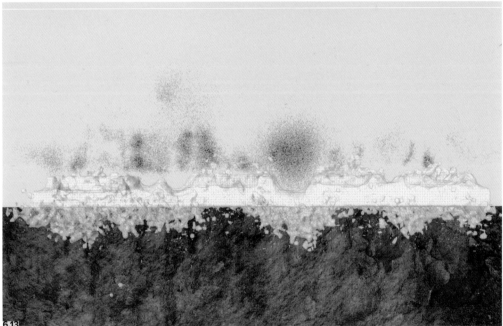

6.13

experience of space, the project atomises painting through
a series of translation 'tools' developed in software. These
are then used to recreate a three dimensional manifestation
of these spaces. As the controlled viewpoint is of utmost
importance to the construction of space, the project takes a
site of interchange near Grand Street station, where the flow of
pedestrian traffic starts to define a series of shifting vistas that
evoke a digitised presence of the landscape painter's 'eye'.

6.14

6.15

6.16

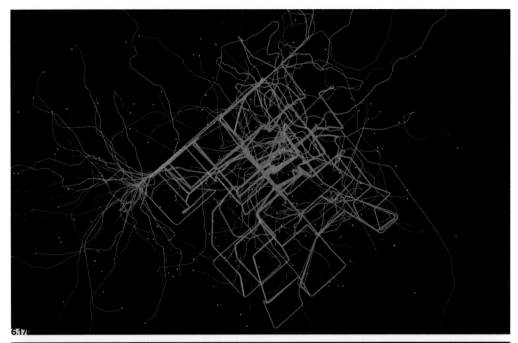

6.17

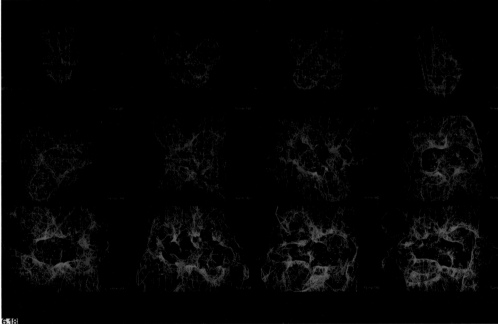

6.18

6.14 – 6.18 Liang Huang Mycelium as Infrastructural Navigator. The project focuses on the growth patterns of the mould mycelium, and the sophisticated way in which it seeks out nutrition and forms into a structure. Using tests to define actual structural formations recorded in photographs, a series of simulations were developed through algorithms to understand the behaviour of mould as a system of expansion and infrastructure for capturing and processing nutrition. The growth properties of nutrition are used to create a system of architectural interventions within disadvantaged blocks within large Chinese cities, where unchecked development and unregulated structures create a built environment with many requirements for amenities and support structures. By placing 'nutrition' points, such as public throroughfares, structural weaknesses in existing buildings, and utility points, mycelium growth is used to derive a superstructure to grow into and formalise these unchecked developments. **6.18** Tests using processing to develop growth pattern algorithms, taking the nature of mycelium and exploiting the nutrition-seeking capabilities of the organism to propose a strategy for linking the city together.

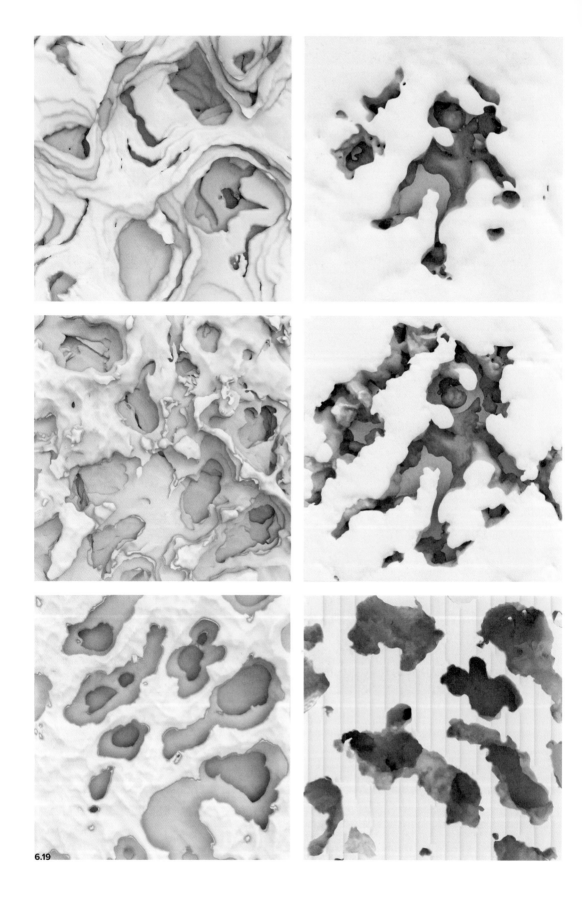

6.19

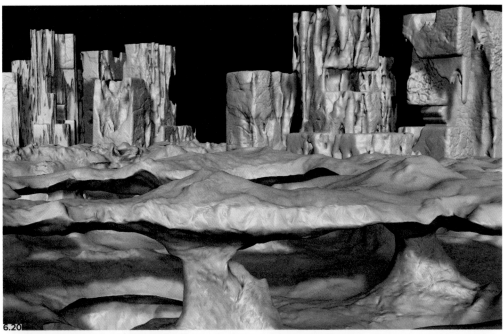

6.20

6.21

6.19 – 6. 20 Yang Yang Regolithic Architectures. Through the simulation of weathering processes, architectural space can be created as the resultant formation of site and contextual conditions. The regolithic top surface of the architectural structure is manipulated by simulated forces and weather conditions, starting to form typologies of space and structural elements within. Developing a storm-proof landscape for Fire Island in Upstate New York, the project proposes that the 'pre-weathered' structure starts to provide buffer zones and strengthened infrastructure for the existing towns in the area. The images show the progressive weathering process and the resultant dissolving of simple monolithic forms into geometries shaped and refined through a progressive application of forces. **6.21 – 6.25 Yuchen Liu** Generative Morphology –

Demolition as design method. A view through a new garden for the Winter Palace in Beijing, where demolished structures are preserved as public amenities rather than being rebuilt into private developments. Through simulation the morphological properties of demolition processes becomes a strategy for deriving architectural form.

6.22

6.23

6.24

6.22 – 6.25 The project investigates the morphological potential of demolition, and how the process of destroying buildings can be simulated and subsequently be applied to a design method. Taking a site at risk near the Winter Palace in Beijing, the project proposes to reimagine the typological spaces of the palace gardens, strewn with ruins, using the raw material of buildings currently planned for demolition by the Chinese government. The simulation was developed through research into industrial demolition techniques, the placement, strength and material composition of explosive charges, and the morphological procedure that buildings subsequently undergo, how precise and yet imprecise this process becomes. As a design method, the simulation allows for spaces to be formed through twisting, rupturing, expanding, fragmenting.

These architectures together constitute new forms of landscape emerging from the geopolitical strain of redevelopment, taking raw materials of waste, and speculating on their morphological potential for deriving new architectural forms.

6.26

6.27

6.26 – 6.31 Ioanna Cheinoporou Non linearity: a Syntactical (Urban) Equilibrium. The project focuses on the manipulation of the city data as the immaterial brick of a recursive procedure which ends up proposing a distributional method of wifi hotspots throughout Central Park as well as their formal manifestation. This designing procedure, which is recursively implemented on sequential scales, is algorithmically guided by the properties of a Spring System which tends to achieve an equilibrium of its elements under any circumstances or alterations of its components. These properties suggest a rearrangement of the city condition through a 'syntactical' redistribution and adjacency of the existing nodes of the built environment and those of the urban tensions which emerge by citizens' behaviours. This process 'reads' the invisible components of the city and metaphorically simulates the interactive relationship between cyberspace and urban reality as a non linear structure. This chaotic non-linearity could be further recognised in the physical and spatial outcome of this procedure, implicated by indeterminate wire structures emerging from the volumisation of the distribution system of the wifi nodes. **6.28** An interior view within one of the structures formed by the volumisation process. Spaces and configurations of behaviour within the system start to define new architectural territories, uses and properties that extend beyond the wifi network into providing programmatic spaces for Central Park. **6.29 – 6.30** Views of typical structures in their Central Park context. The system generates components such as the wifi tower, but also produces emanations from this

6.28

6.29

6.30

process that become larger architectural interventions with
enclosure and occupiable space distributed across the park
to create a new landscape of elements.

6.31 Drawing showing the formation of a structure through
the syntactical network coaslescing and assembling nodal
points into architectural forms. The system is scalable so that
the network that defines the larger architectural forms can
also be applied to manifesting furniture, surface treatment
and structural solutions within the wider distribution.
By programming different behaviours into the system,
this scalability can be further manipulated to produce a
network that defines different types of architectural forms
across Central Park, public structures that vary in scale and
programmatic possibility.

6.32

6.32 – 6.34 Yi-Chiao Huang Manhattan New(t) Skin Project. Hurricane Sandy, a powerful tropical cyclone that devastated New York years ago, has stirred the attention of relevant government agencies about the increasing flood risk. The project imagines that experimental secret projects have already been initiated, the most peculiar one named 'Manhattan New(t) Skin Project'. The project looked at porosity and skin as a typological approach for a permeable landscape designed to manipulate flood water. Investigating novel applications of soft material and adaptive systems led to the production of an architectural strategy that eschews the typical 'solidity' of flood defence systems. The properties of Newt skin were explored to create an approach to a structure that not only involves permeable layers, but has the potential for metamorphosis across the linespace of the structure, much as the infant and adult newt skin deals with water in remarkably different ways. The project examined systems of membranes and layers, and how they could manipulate the flow of water, proposing that this is then applied to the existing city in the form of a combinatory and sacrificial flood defence system located on the tip of Manhattan Island (Battery Park), with multifunctional layers and membranes, inflatable barriers and landscapes. Tested through flow modelling software, these structures slow down and redirect flood water to underground lakes and rivers, and during the process transform the energy of flowing water and thermal heat into electricity and steam for city's use.

6.33

6.341

Research
Cluster

7

Gamescapes

Jose Sanchez

The Bartlett School of Architecture 2013

'Decisions are singular and unrepeatable; they cannot be generalised into rules. But all this also means that we cannot say that decision simply "emerges" out of a chaotic background, or pops out thanks to the movement from one "basin of attraction" to another. No self-organising system can obviate the need for such a decision, or dictate what it will be. And decision always implies novelty or difference – in this way it is absolutely incompatible with notions of autopoiesis, homeostasis, or Spinoza's conatus. What we need is an aesthetics of decision, instead of our current metaphysics of emergence.' Steven Shaviro

Architecture Stuck with Itself

The role of computation and digital design practices in the past 20 years has focused on ideas of form generation and manufacturing, emphasising the empirical performance of design and leading towards a convergent notion of optimum. The increasing use of computer simulation software grows towards a megalomania of forecasting, anticipating spatial and formal outcomes. It is precisely this context from which totalising discourses of architecture could emerge, overarching and overriding the different approaches and design strategies still present in our design milieu.

The proliferation of computational virtuosity in the realm of design has been in the service of the few starchitects who can profit from and exploit these alienated models of knowledge. The continuous training of new proletarians, equipped with robotic arms and laser scanners, can only reach an inevitable collapse.

While the study of complexity in different fields has led to replace a reductionist model, the embrace of complexity studies in architecture has been paradoxical. For the most part, it seems to imply direct relation with form: complex system = complex formal answer. The use of biological analogies and references to nature seem to redeem the architect from all responsibility of judgment and decision-making, providing the ultimate alibi for the exploration of form.

Open Architecture Models as a Form of Research In May 2008, David Baker and his team released Foldit, a computer game based on real scientific models that allows players to engage with protein folding solutions. Within days the game achieved solutions to puzzles at the edge of scientific knowledge. The crowdsourcing approach to problemsolving proves to be smarter than state-of-the-art algorithms. Foldit has been recognised as a canonical example of the potential of video games for research, but its puzzle model is still based on an idea of a 'solution' or 'optimum'. In May 2009, Markus Persson released Minecraft, an open sandbox game. The unexpected response to Persson's system of digital permutations and open game mechanics has become a paradigm shift in the world of game design. The user search space is infinitely vast, described by very simple discrete rules. The economy of relations and permutations of objects is a constant drive for design and creation.

Rigorous Engines and Intuitive Gameplay

Research Cluster 7 embarked on the design of procedural sandbox games in which the systems of relations establish a rigorous understanding of architectural variables yet allow for an intuitive gameplay or 'search-space' of different configurations. The cluster used a theoretical framework of Object Oriented Ontology, looking at authors like Ian Bogost and Timothy Morton, in the speculation of a flat ontological status between humans and objects, both physical and conceptual. The game design agenda required the study of game theory and interface design, as well as the collection of data sets from players' experience. The Cluster aimed to produce an operational game by the end of the year, where the design agenda could be understood through gameplay. Games have been made available online for data collection and research analysis, and can be downloaded and played at: www.plethora-project.com/studio

Based on a model of Human-Computer cooperation, the Cluster seeks to bring back intuition to the world of algorithmic design. The game medium seeks to develop a non-unified framework for design, where difference is celebrated not equalised; to replace notions of parametric search with crowd computing; and to engage design space as a form of research.

Computer / Human Interface – Generative Models

In Term 1 the Cluster studied the relation between generative models and human interaction. Looking at discrete geometrical models like Conaway's 'Game of Life', students learned the use of neighbour calculations to establish a system of transactions. The outcomes were delivered as a simple applet with basic notions of interactivity and decision-making.

Architecture in conflict – Game Theory

The Cluster looked at an architectural scenario in terms of conflict. von Neumann's notions of game theory were the framework to understand the conflict of form in a larger socio-political context. We engaged with notions of value and 'panchromatic scoring' presenting the information in a 'prisoner's dilemma' format.

SandBox – Gamescapes – Social Computing

Finally, we allowed students to flesh out their game proposal as a thesis, developing in detail the tuning of rule systems and notions of values explored in past terms. Early prototypes of the game were released in order to develop data collection as a feedback mechanism of the core game mechanics. The architectural objects present in the game were designed and presented in detail, explaining the data and rules that govern them in a larger object choreography.

Students
Dimitra Angelopoulou, Vasiliki Diamanti, Xuan Guo, Meropi Karantaki, Efthymia Dimitra Kotsani, Georgios Tsakiridis, Ying Xiao

Project teams
Re.On Efthymia Dimitra Kotsani, Georgios Tsakiridis
Wireflies Dimitra Angelopoulou, Vasiliki Diamanti, Meropi Karantaki
Breath Xuan Guo, Ying Xiao

7.1

7.2

7.1 – 7.7 Re.On This project explores coastal structures with the inherent ability to harvest and purify seawater. Its goal is the reconsideration of the infrastructure of water and the exploration of its ability to create architectural narratives and produce space through the development of a game platform.
7.2 Dealing with water creates connotations related to the water management issues and the forthcoming global water crisis. Speculations on the redefinition of the existing building blocks of architecture, specifically water architecture, led to the proposal of sandbox consisting of a predefined type and number of elements (distribution components, desalinators) that could be combined (and re-combined) in multiple assemblages. A future application in the context of under-developed or developing countries and the harvesting of water

as a function itself could potentially create a micro-economy that is related either to the maintenance of its inhabitants or its own existence (regarding its maintenance or expansion).
7.3 The main goal of the game is the development of structures which are able to absorb seawater, filter and desalinate it and eventually use it for storage and cultivation of the surrounding environment. The research begins with the study of a typical L-system for the generation of the basic units, intending to speculate on matters of orientation and the exploration of the element of flexibility as a basic attribute of the system. Through the introduction of character animation techniques (rigging) the units are able to deform in various shapes and configurations, arguing about a component made of flexible material with soft rubber-like joints.

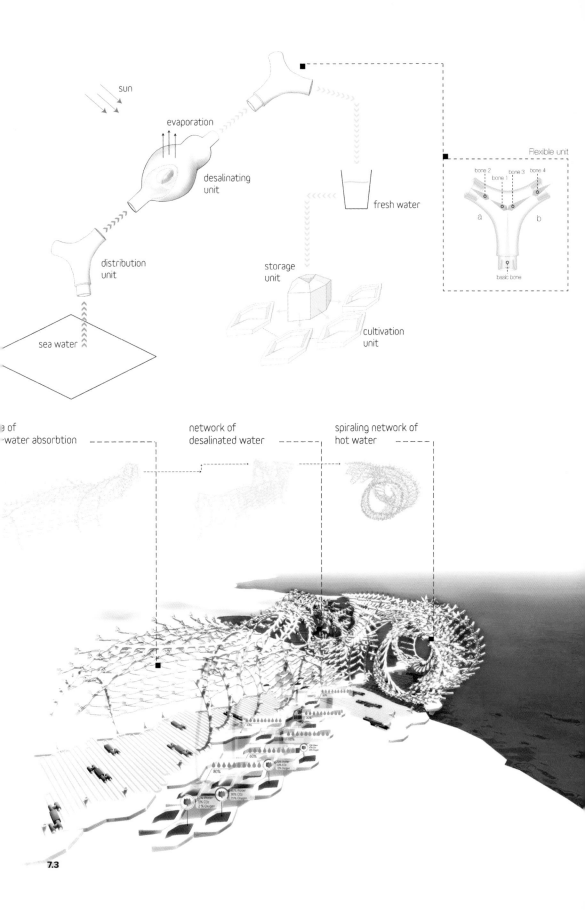

sun

evaporation

desalinating
unit

distribution
unit

fresh water

sea water

storage
unit

cultivation
unit

Flexible unit

bone 2 bone 1 bone 3 bone 4

a   b

basic bone

e of
-water absorbtion

network of
desalinated water

spiraling network of
hot water

7.3

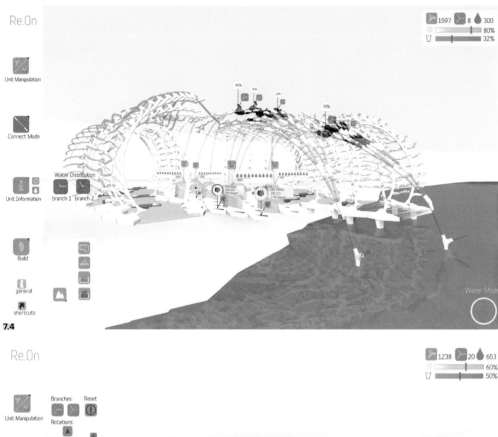

7.4

7.5

7.4 Although someone could argue that the computation could be achieved through all sort of different algorithmic design platforms, what seems to be the fundamental element in this approach is the interface: the layer of information that regulates the communication or 'symbiosis' between the user/designer/player and the algorithm itself and takes advantage of the game mechanics by presenting the information at the moment of decisionmaking and not after, as a post-rational process. **7.5** The question that emerges is: how the distribution of water from unit to unit would influence the design decision, and consequently, the morphology of the outcome. While, the algorithm itself allows the units to talk to each other, making them aware of their neighbours, the live projection of the information through the interface enables an instant 'reading'

of the data from the user. An overlaying system of information is introduced, focusing mainly on the water aspects of the project and also the elements of the surrounding environment (sun exposure, cultivation, etc). **7.6** Instance of one of the multiple outcomes that evolve through gameplay. In parallel to the accomplishment of what seems the major task, which is the absorption and filtration of seawater to produce fresh water, the user has the ability to generate complex spatial formations that could potentially evolve into architecture.

76

7.7

7.7 The evolving architecture does not intend to give a
definitive answer, rather to open a spectrum of probabilities
through the various configurations of components.
Re-assemby evolves as the main methodology to discover
meaningful outcomes out of all the possible combinations.
Through this research, the project investigates the potential
architecture that could emerge on the blurring boundaries
between the land and the sea, functioning as an actuator,
which influences both the relationship of the structural
space with its environment, and also the relations which are
developed among the environmental elements themselves.

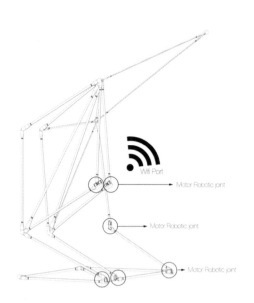

circle beh

up-down beh

wave beh

loop beh

vertical fol

follower

robot-human

human(num)

human(height)

7.8

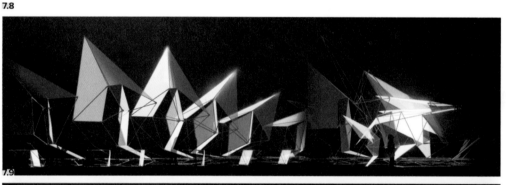

7.9

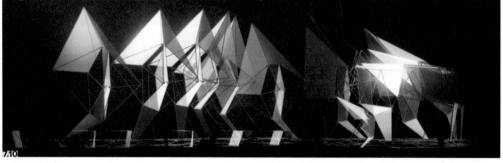

7.10

7.8 – 7.17 Breath Generating complex behaviours from simple interaction of human and robotic joints. **7.8** Icons represent behaviours in the game: red icons are motion behaviours, which are independent. Blue icons are relation behaviours, which follow other joints. Green icons are for the behaviours between robotic joints and human: the distance, the number and the height of human are inputs of behaviours. Sensors and a wifi-port are embedded in the frame. **7.9** An architectural product kit, which works both on the interior and exterior. It could be a temporary market or music event shelter. Complex behaviours provide different spatial qualities for the space it inhabits. **7.10** The movement of this space configuration. Colour lines show the type of network and icons show the behaviours. For instance, wave motion is independent

behaviour, allowing the frame to move both forward/backward and up/down, and does not need other frames as an input. Follower behaviour is dependent: it will learn or follow other frames, and creates lag from the frame it learns. **7.11 – 7.13** The digital network - the data visualisation of robotic behaviours - describes the learning path players build and explains relationships. It is visible only in the game, but based on real occurrences. For instance, the network topology in 7.11 means one node is moving and being followed by others. 7.13 shows the interaction between the 'star' and 'cross' networks.

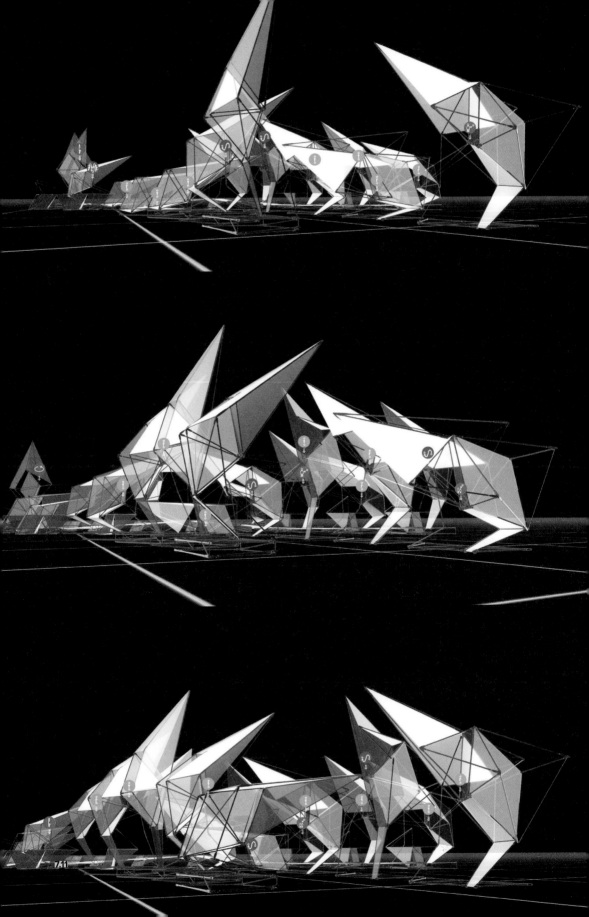

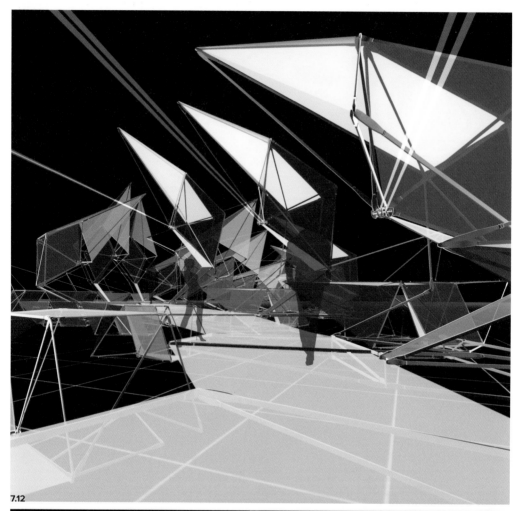

7.12

7.13

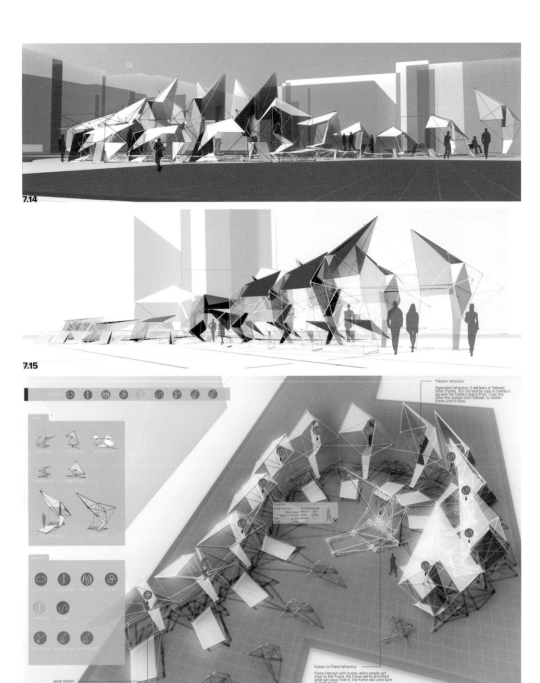

7.14

7.15

7.16

7.14 – 7.15 Game scenes. The interface is a key design tool and the key point of game algorithm is player. Therefore, in game mechanics, the design guides the players to produce more outcomes with various performances. **7.16** Game interface, allowing players to drag and drop behaviours and frames. Information about the relationship between frame agents overlays with the movement of frames visible in the real world. Robotic joints are like the 'brain' of architecture that can respond to data both from humans and other intelligent joints. The highlight frame is activated when people get close to it. In the game environment, players can see this invisible data, which helps them understand the complex system.

7.17

7.17 Based on the game mechanics, the project explores architectural design with the notion of digital materiality and physical symbiosis. Though a sandbox of behaviours, the Breath project provides novel views of lifelike structures and makes the transition between structure and architectural space meaningfully. Social engagement, material and space economy and energy consumption are presented in the project.

Click Actuater

vertical fol   follower   robot-human   human(num)   human(height)

Diagram Mode

Sliders

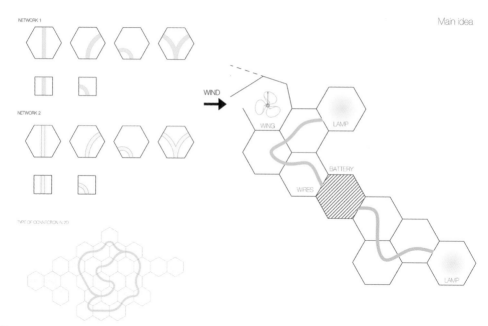

NETWORK 1

NETWORK 2

TYPE OF CONNECTION IN 2D

WIND

WING

LAMP

BATTERY

WIRES

LAMP

7.18

7.19

7.18 – 7.25 Wireflies Exploring the potential for creating an architectural system through a playful design process. It is about the creative expression of users, who explore new strategies in architectural design through decisionmaking. The Wireflies game explores new building blocks of architecture working around the collection of wind energy and its distribution. Players can use light patterns to intuitively redefine the topology of the circuits and information networks that run through the building fabric. **7.18** Diagram representing the main idea of capturing and transferring the wind inside the system. **7.19** Digital representation of the Wireflies system (image taken from the game play). The lighting patterns visualise information indicating the existence and the directionality of the electricity as well as the availability

of the system to provide electricity for use. **7.20** A different configuration result from the game. The idea of the Wireflies system is to create an open sandbox video game as a discrete kit of parts that could be assembled and disassembled resulting in different aggregations. **7.21** An important element of the Wireflies system is the use of the interface as a way to communicate the game with the public and put the player on the same level as the game components. The game's interface allows the player to choose between the different components, place them in the game canvas and assign them a different behaviour according to user's decisionmaking.

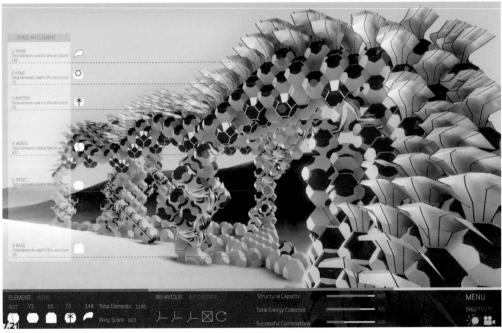

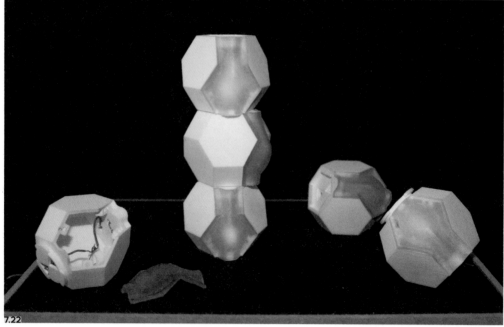

7.22

1 WIND

2. ELECTRICITY

3. PATTERN

ELEMENT

BEHAVIOUR

Structural Capacity

Total Energy Collected

Successful Combinations

MENU

SHORTCUTS

Total Elements

Wing Score

7.23

7.22 Based on kit assembly concepts, the physical representation of Wireflies' system suggests the communication of units in a local coordinate system, the project implements computation in the construction process. Components' discrete connections allow for a passing of information between them, or else a 'digital' communication. In the physical model the energy/electricity flows through the network of wires, the copper connections enable the conductivity and transfer of data, while the LED infrastructure indicates the transmission and creates a glowing pattern. The components are kept together with magnetic connections. **7.23** Wind is the main element of Wireflies' system. The collection of wind contributes to the design process and helps the architectural configuration as it triggers the expression of

the façade of the building in an ecological and economic way. Wing components can open up in the air, expand in order to channel and guide the air inside the component. They are designed to work like a funnel, in order to concentrate more wind in a smaller space. The wings' elastic deformation captures the air and through a mechanism (turbine) that is placed inside the component, converts the kinetic energy of motion into electricity. Wings start from discrete truncated octahedron units and when they open up they begin blurring the geometry, going from one unit to the whole, from a series of components to one piece. **7.24** Top view of a Wireflies configuration and the set of components that are used. The wings capture the air, while the open components bring it to the inside of the structure, creating a porous fabric.

7.24

These components constitute an interactive system that is
not only a beautiful aesthetic addition, but also convey a vast
amount of information regarding the environment. In addition,
the are evolve from self-contained devices to highly dynamic
systems, which are interconnected with the surrounding
environment. **7.25** Game information, details of components'
values can be represented to the player while playing the
game, regarding the amount of wind collection, energy saved
and energy consumed. A system of evaluation has been
implemented in order to motivate the user.

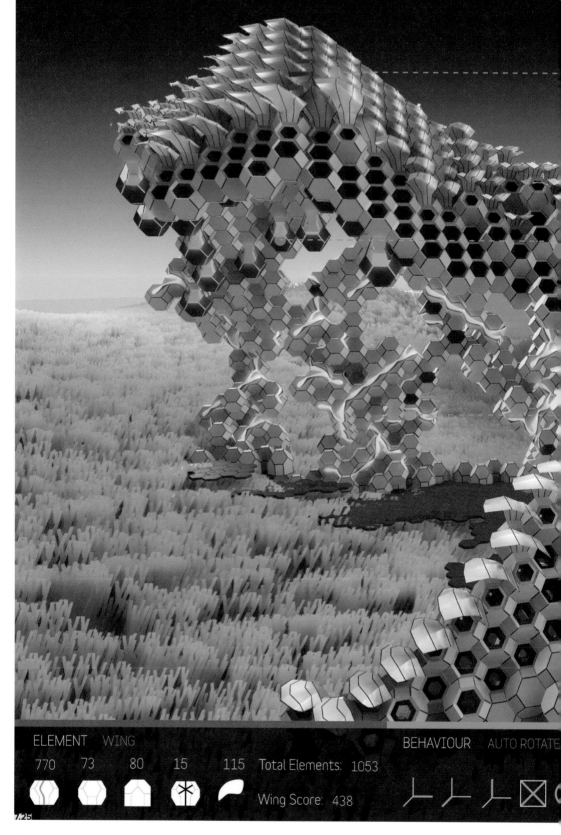

The Bartlett School of Architecture 2013

ELEMENT   WING

770   73   80   15   115   Total Elements: 1053

Wing Score: 438

BEHAVIOUR   AUTO ROTATE

7.25

Wing_Total Energy Produced

Each wing has the ability to produce 100V by capturing the wind. For better efficiency higher places are preferred.

Battery_Total Energy Collected

Each battery has the ability to store around 1000V by collecting energy from the wings. Their placement should be done strategically because of their restricted number.

Wires_Total Energy Consumed

Each wire consumes around 300V. Consequently, every component needs at least 3 wings to lihgt up.

Structural Capacity	430
Total Energy Collected	500
Successful Combinations	155

MENU

SHORTCUTS

Research
Cluster

Crafting Space

Daniel Widrig

Hailed as Industrial Revolution 2.0, digital fabrication, particularly additive manufacturing, has long impacted industries that are traditionally faster in adapting to new technologies such as fashion, product and automotive design. Those industries not only actively engage in the development of these new techniques but already managed to fully integrate technologies such as 3D printing not only for prototyping or product development but for the manufacturing of market ready products. Brands like Audi for instance use PolyJet technology to build final large-scale car parts that before required complex and expensive moulds. In other cases, additive manufacturing is used to directly print moulds, eliminating the exorbitant cost of traditional mould-making. These are just two examples from a large pool of possibilities of using new materialisation techniques in an opportunistic way.

In contrast to this, in an architectural context rapid prototyping still propagates and is reduced to being a fast and painless way of creating representational models instead of using its potential for architectural production and to bring a new materiality into the architect's increasingly virtual studio. This is at least partly due to the fact that until recently only larger commercial practices and institutions were in a position to acquire expensive equipment. The recent plunging of cost of industrial-quality manufacturing tools as well as and the general democratisation of tools (soft- and hardware) is changing this. The spread of open source/DIY equipment, shared knowledge and innovation in the bypassing of patents – both in terms of machine construction as well as the production of consumables – now basically allows to create complex parts for free and enables also smaller studios to engage with these systems.

In that context, Research Cluster 8 engages a new kind of craft, rooted in a thorough understanding of traditional, hands-on craft combined with an expertise in contemporary computational concepts.

The studio is particularly interested in combining traditional, low-tech manufacturing processes with advanced technological approaches to design and realise new spatial concepts. Set up as an open framework, the Cluster allows students to script individual architectural scenarios and address those through custom form-finding and materialisation processes. The emerging proposals (prototypical structures, architectural objects and products) are built and tested at a 1:1 scale.

Thanks to Alisa Andrasek, Saffet Kaya Bekiroglu, Stephen Gage, Someen Hahm, Tobias Klein, Ross Lovegrove, Frédéric Migayrou, Igor Pantic, Andrew Porter, Jose Sanchez, David Scott.

Students
Stefan Bassing, Bernardo Pedro Dias, Lauren Diaz, Sowmya Mahesh, Matt Martensen, Efstratia Orfanou, Chiaki Yatsui, Qiuying Zhong

Project teams
Ara[x]nes Stefan Bassing, Matt Martensen, Efstratia Orfanou, Qiuying Zhong
IN / OF / FROM Bernardo Pedro Dias, Lauren Diaz, Sowmya Mahesh and Chiaki Yatsui
Timescape Bernardo Pedro Dias, Chiaki Yatsui and Qiuying Zhong
Vertical Belay Matt Martensen, Efstratia Orfanou

8.1 – 8.4 Ara[x]nes 8.1 Large-scale prototype assembly.
8.2 Installation view. **8.3** Steps of fabrication process (assembly
of wooden framework, weaving of threads within framework,
laminating and removal of emerging component structure
from framework). **8.4** Digital prototype of proposed installation.

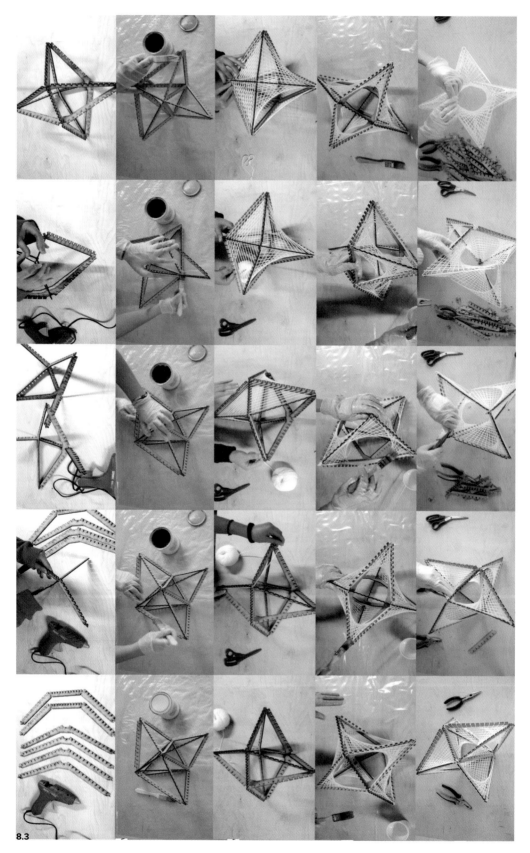

8.3

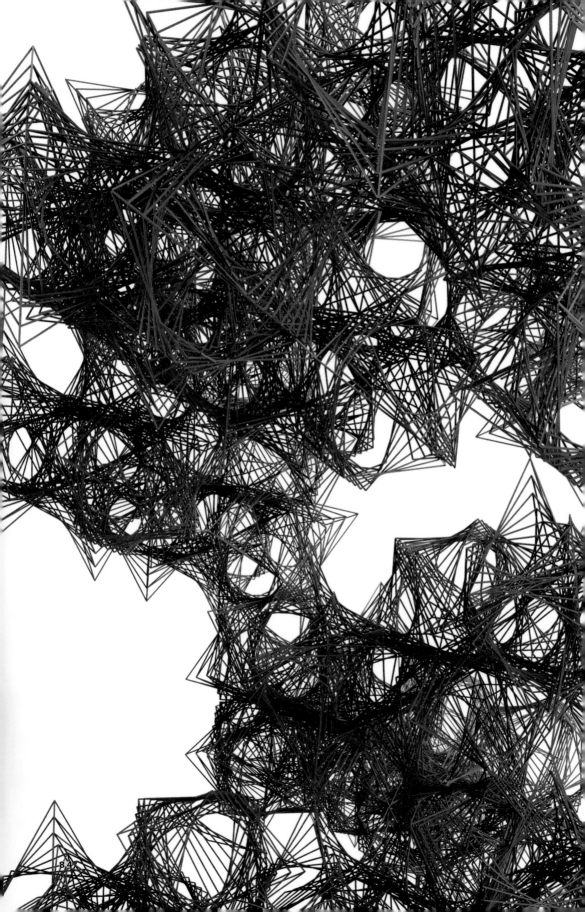

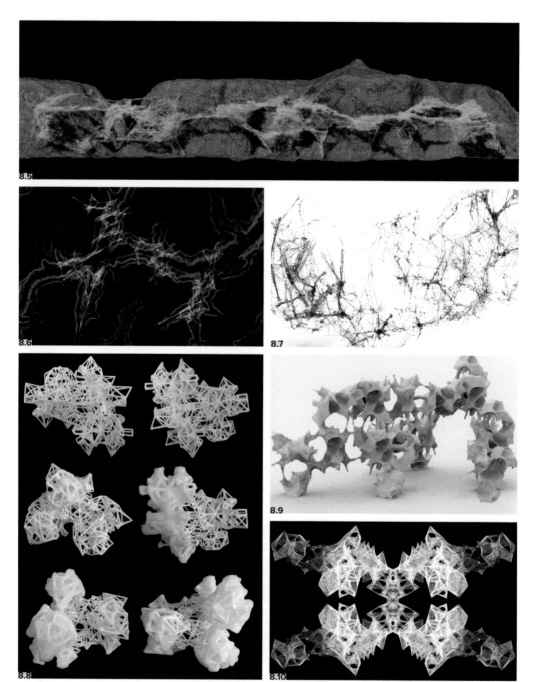

8.5 – 8.7 Vertical Belay 8.5 Elevation (Grand Canyon, USA).
8.6 Diagrammatic top view (Grand Canyon, USA). **8.7** Digital
simulation of thread and fibre system. **8.8 – 8.9 Sowmya
Mahesh** Transcending Permanence **8.8** Wax as a dipping
medium coats 3D-printed prototypes. With successive layers
of wax the structure gradually changes from mesh to solid,
creating differentiated zones of varying densities. **8.9**
Perspective view of a proposed pavilion. The digital model is
generated based on conclusions drawn from analogue dipping
experiments. **8.10 Ara[x]nes** Physical model showing transition
and various densities. **8.11 Vertical Belay** Perspective view of
proposal showing connections between cliffs and structure
and possible recreational spaces for climbers (Grand Canyon,
USA).

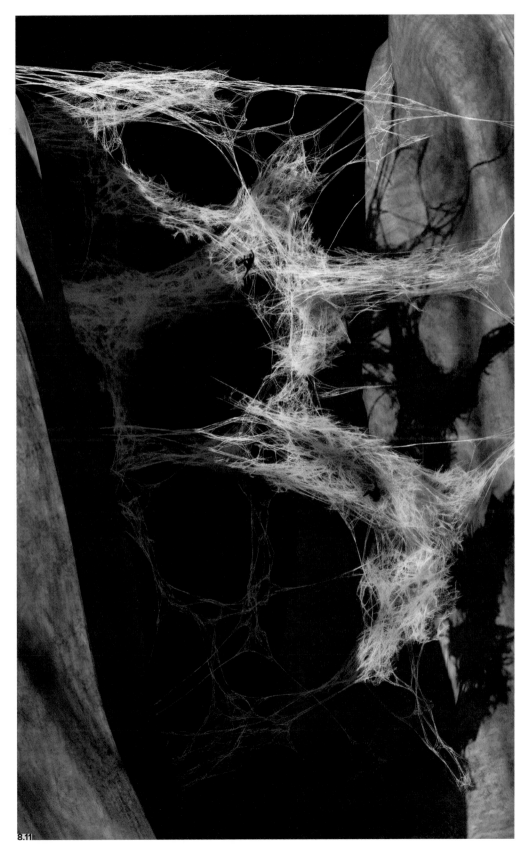

8.11

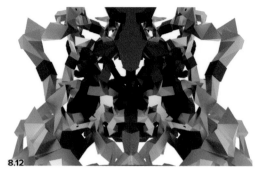

8.12

8.13

8.14

8.15

8.12 – 8.18 IN/OF/FROM 8.12 – 8.13 Furniture scale
multi-material studies using series of solid and hollow bricks.
8.14 – 8.15 Architectural scale scenario using hollow and
branched components. This project aimed to build 1:1
industrial strength building components using customised 3D
printers assembled by students at the beginning of the term.
The printers were used to directly produce bricks as well as to
produce moulds which were used to create additional
components through concrete and foam casting.

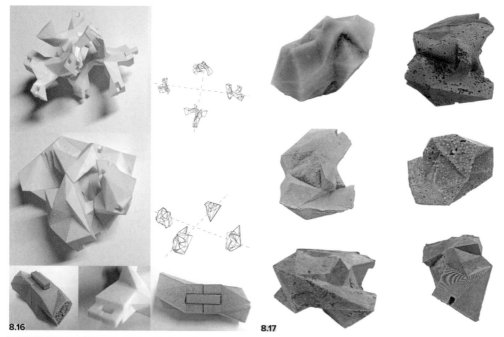

8.16 3D-printed interlocking components and joints.
8.17 Various components made from wax, concrete, foam and concrete-styrofoam mixtures produced to understand material systems with regards to porosity, weight, economy, and structural performance. **8.18** Full-scale prototype combining 3D-printed pieces with concrete cast parts.

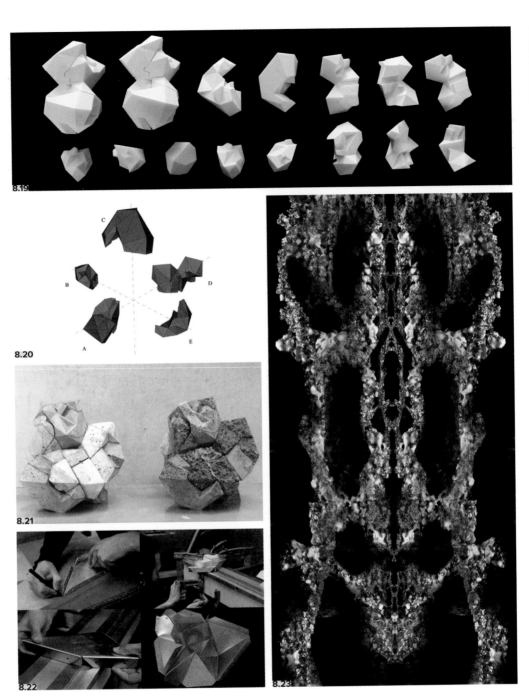

8.19 – 8.27 Timescape 8.19 Catalogue of self-interlocking components (Stereolitography/SLS). **8.20** Assembly manual / diagram of interlocking units. **8.21** States of erosion (1:1 scale multi-material prototype). **8.22** Mould production employing waterjet cutting and metal folding. **8.23** Conceptual section.

8.24

8.25

8.26

8.24 Aggregation of components and scale approach to
site. The sketch explores possiblities to combine various
geometric typologies within one architectural artefact.
8.25 Site plan (Coimbra, Portugal). **8.26** Erosion patterns.
8.27 Transitions between smooth and sharp elements emerge
through different degrees of erosion driven by the deployment
of materials with varying properties. Materials range from
lasting fibre-reinforced concrete to porous concrete-earth
mixtures to decomposing cork.

8.28

8.29

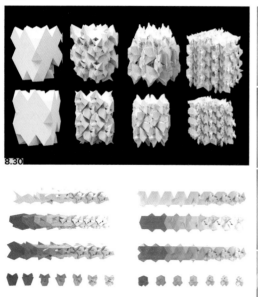

8.30

8.31

8.32

8.28 – 8.29 Lauren Diaz High/Low : Low/High Complex
Diagram of building component's packing strategies derived
from the interior of a bisymmetrical hendecahedron changing
in levels of resolution. Higher resolution sections are used for
porous architectural functions (ventilation, egress) while lower
resolution bricks are used for structural integrity, resulting in
a cohesive design strategy between aesthetic, construction,
and functional qualities. **8.30 – 8.32 Lauren Diaz** Squish
Bricks. 1:1 building components made from an inflated silicone
rubber skin and filled with air or other material ranging in
firmness and weight, assembled model.

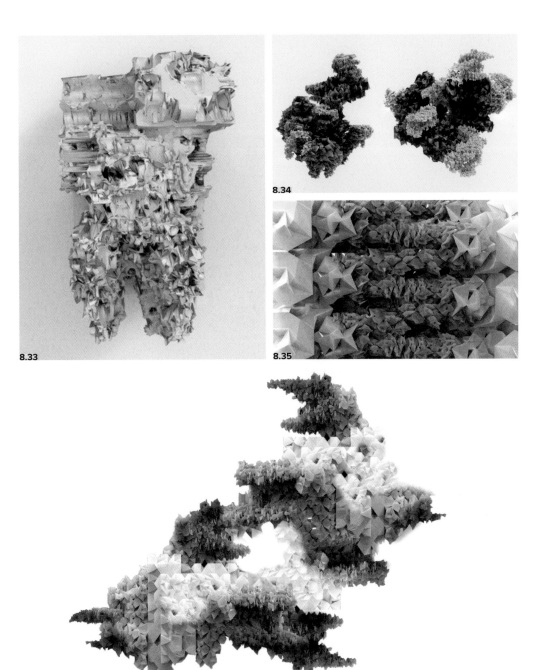

8.34

8.33

8.35

8.36

8.33 – 8.36 Lauren Diaz High/Low : Low/High Complex.
The aggregated components range in scale and resolution
affect the look of the architectural function. Additions can be
annexed as the housing complex grows in numbers seamlessly
by following the packing accretion like packing strategy.

8.37

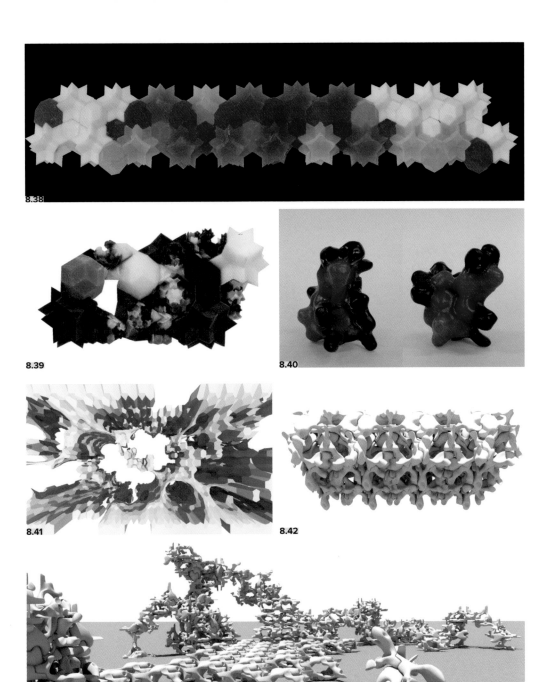

8.37 – 8.41 Stefan Bassing Deep Texture. **8.37** Diagrammatic exploration of transitions within high-resolution architectural fabric. **8.38** Full-scale, multi-material prototype. **8.39** Material sample (Objet multi-material print). **8.40** Material sample (Paraffin). **8.41** Spatial exploration. **8.42 – 8.46 Stefan Bassing** SevenScenarios. **8.42** Dense packing study. **8.43** Project Scenario 'Sculpture Garden'.

8.44

8.45

8.46

8.44 Various studies of structural typologies. **8.45** Project
Scenario 'Cantilever'. **8.46** Diagrammatic Section.
8.47 Timescape Conceptual Section.

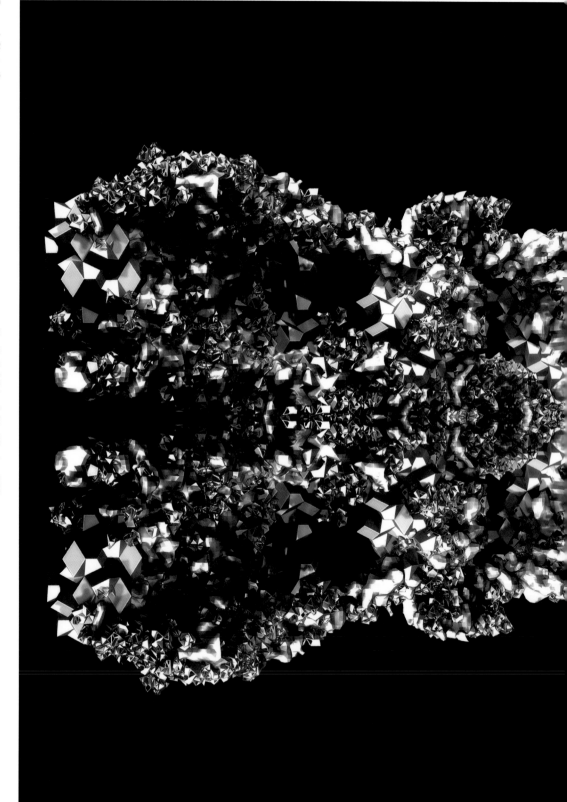

8.47

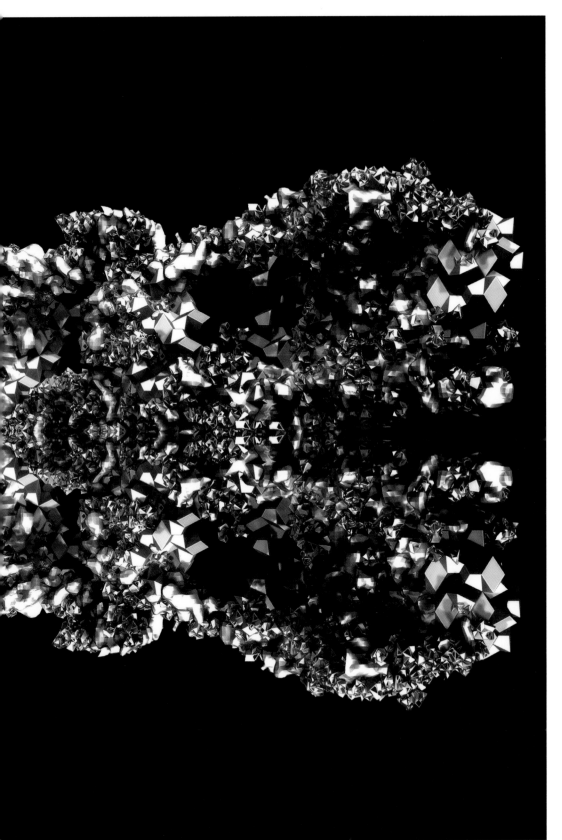

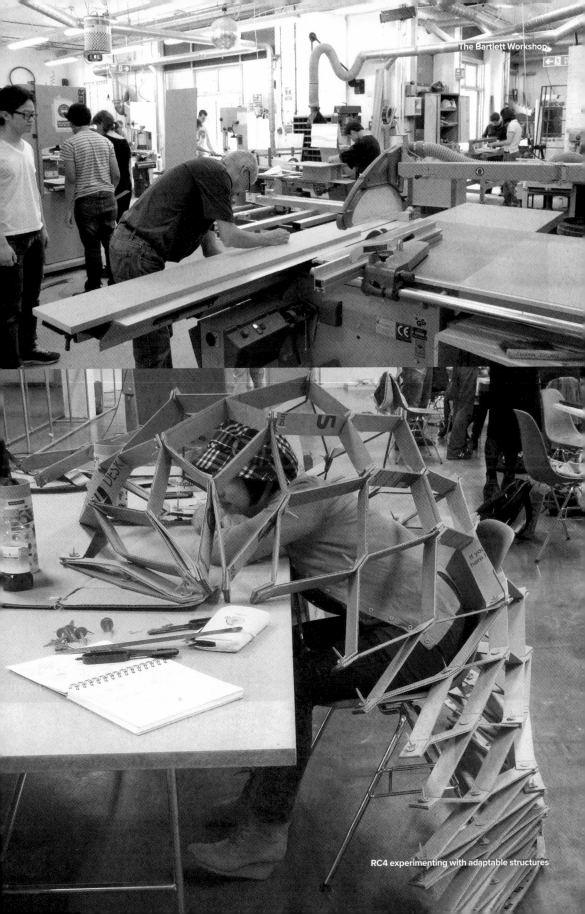

RC4 experimenting with adaptable structures

fletcher priest architects
trust

www.fletcherpriest.com

Bartlett Lectures

The Bartlett International Lecture Series
features speakers from across the world.
Lectures in the series are open to the public
and free to attend.

This year's speakers included:

Rob Adams
Ben Addy
Yannis Aesopos
Ben van Berkel
Aaron Betsky
Iain Borden
Benjamin Bratton
Mario Carpo
Peter Cook
Nat Chard
Raffaello D'Andrea
Graham Harman
Jonathan Hill
Luca Galofaro
Giuseppe Longo
Kengo Kuma
Winy Maas
Gurjit Singh Matharoo
Achim Menges
Nicholas de Monchaux
Gianni Pettena
Dominique Perrault
Wolfgang Rieder
Joseph Rykwert
Philippe Rahm
Casey Reas
Jenny E Sabin
Bob Sheil
Kristina Schinegger and Stefan Rutzinger
Tezuka Takaharu
Timothy Wray and Andrew Higgott

The Bartlett International Lecture Series is
generously sponsored by the Fletcher Priest Trust.

A new range of smaller lecture series' attracted over
50 speakers to our Royal Ear Hospital building.

Bartlett Nexus
Maj Plemenitas, Gennaro Senatore, Ezio Blasetti,
Paul Nicholls, Tobias Klein, Madhav Kidao, Jack
Munro, Michail Desyllas, Gregory Epps, Kate Davies,
Slub, Catrina Stewart, Tom Betts, Matt Johnson, Ollie
Palmer, Manja van de Worp, Marcus Wendt and
Vera-Maria Glahn, Memo Akten, Mollie Claypool,
Ines Dantas, Niccolo Casas, Martin Dittus, Cohen
Van Balen, Vlad Tenu, Gilles Retsin, Ryan Mehanna,
Tom Smith

Effective Knowledge
Emilie Hergott, Nicolas Bredeche, Justin
Dirrenberger, Andrew Witt, Lucia Mondardini,
Niccolo Baldasssini

Material Matters
Daniel Bosa, Enrico Dini, Matt Wade, Ollie Palmer

Bartlett lectures can be viewed at
vimeo.com/bartlettarchucl

Staff

Professor Frédéric Migayrou
Bartlett Professor of
Architecture, Chair
B-Pro Director

Dr Marcos Cruz
Reader in Architecture
Director of School

Professors

Professor Peter Bishop
Professor of Urban Design

Professor Iain Borden
Professor of Architecture
& Urban Culture
Vice Dean of Communications
Director of History & Theory

Professor Adrian Forty
Professor of Architectural
History
MA Architectural History
Programme Director

Professor Colin Fournier
Professor of Urban Design

Professor Murray Fraser
Professor of Architecture
& Global Culture
Vice Dean of Research

Professor Stephen Gage
Professor of Innovative
Technology

Professor Christine Hawley
Professor of Architectural
Studies
Director of Design

Professor Jonathan Hill
Professor of Architecture
& Visual Theory
MPhil/PhD by Design
Programme Director

Professor CJ Lim
Professor of Architecture
& Cultural Design
Vice Dean of International
Affairs

Professor Jane Rendell
Professor of Architecture & Art
Vice Dean of Research

Professor Bob Sheil
Professor of Architecture and
Design through Production
Director of Technology and
Computing

Academic Staff

Laura Allen
Senior Lecturer
BSc Architecture Programme
Director

Alisa Andrasek
Lecturer in Advanced
Architectural Computation
MArch GAD Programme
Leader

Julia Backhaus
MArch Architecture
Programme Director

Dr Jan Birksted
Principal Research Associate
Coordinator Year 3 History &
Theory

Matthew Butcher
Lecturer in Architecture and
Performance
Coordinator of Pedagogic
Affairs

Dr Ben Campkin
Lecturer in History & Theory
Director of Urban Lab

Dr Marjan Colletti
Senior Lecturer
Acting MArch Architecture
Programme Director

Ruairi Glynn
Lecturer in Interactive
Architecture

Dr Penelope Haralambidou
Lecturer in Architecture
Coordinator of MPhil / PhD by
Design

Dirk Krolikowski
Lecturer in Innovative
Technology & Design Practice
Associate Coordinator of Year
4 Design Realisation

Dr Adrian Lahoud
Reader in Urban Design
MArch UD Programme Leader

Dr Yeoryia Manolopoulou
Senior Lecturer
Director of Architectural
Research

James O'Leary
Lecturer in Innovative
Technology & Design Practice
Coordinator of Year 4 Design
Realisation

Dr Barbara Penner
Senior Lecturer
BSc Architectural Studies
Programme Director
MPhil/PhD History & Theory
Programme Director

Frosso Pimenides
Senior Lecturer
BSc Architecture Year 1
Director

Andrew Porter
B-Pro Deputy Director

Dr Peg Rawes
Senior Lecturer
Associate Director of
Architectural Research

Dr Tania Sengupta
Lecturer in Architectural
History & Theory
Coordinator of Year 2 / Year 4
History & Theory

Mark Smout
Senior Lecturer
Acting Director of Technology
and Computing

Susan Ware
Sub-Dean and Faculty Tutor
Director of Professional
Studies
Part 3 Programme Director

Patrick Weber
Senior Lecturer
BSc Architecture Year 1
Director

Research Fellows & Visiting Professors

Niall McLaughlin
Visiting Professor

Dr Hilary Powell
Research Fellow

Professional Services

**Academic Services
Administration**
Rachael Burnett
Michelle Bush
Emer Girling
Tom Mole

Research
Luis Rego

Communications and Website
Laura Cherry
Jean Garrett
Michelle Lukins

Finance and HR
Sarah Clegg
Stoll Michael
Sheetal Saujani

Professional Studies
Kim Macneill
Indigo Rohrer
Naz Siddique

Facilities
Graeme Kennett
John Riley
Dave Yates

B-Made
Abi Abdolwahabi
Martin Avery
Sarat Babu
Richard Beckett
Matt Bowles
Bim Burton
Inigo Dodd
Justin Goodyer
Richard Grimes
Edgardo de Lara
Robert Randall
Paul Smoothy
Emmanuel Vercruysse
Martin Watmough

MArch GAD Staff

Professor Frédéric Migayrou
B-Pro Director

Andrew Porter
B-Pro Deputy Director

Alisa Andrasek
Programme Leader

Research Cluster Tutors

RC1
Alisa Andrasek
Daghan Cam
Maj Plemenitas

RC2
Marjan Colletti
Pavlos Fereos
Guan Lee

RC3
Ruairi Glynn

RC4
Xavier de Kestelier

RC5
Philippe Morel
Thibault Schwarz

RC6
Luke Pearson

RC7
Jose Sanchez

RC8
Daniel Widrig

History & Theory

Report Coordinator
Professor Stephen Gage

Report Tutors
David Andreen
Daniel Bosia
Kristijan Cebzan
Hannes Mayer
Sam McElhinney
Bruce Davison
David Scott

External Examiners

Professor Matias del Campo
Professor Evan Douglis
Professor Christian Girard
Marta Male-Alemany

Critics and Consultants

Yota Adilenidou
Suzy Antinow
Alessandro Ayuso
Niccolo Baldassini
Paul Bavister
Saffet Kaya Bekiroglu
Nicolas Bredeche
Jason Bruges
Emma Bush
Ben Cerveny
Angelos Chronis
Carole Collet
Sam Conran
Regine Debatty
Bernadette Devilat
David Di Duca
Justin Dirrenberger
Pavlos Fereos
Emmett Glynn
Fred Guttfield
Someen Hahm
Sean Hanna
Alex Haw
Ben Haworth
Jethro Hon
Alvin Huang
Sam Joyce
Zoi Karagkiozi
Tobias Klein
Petros Koutsolampros
Dirk Krolikowski
Diony Kypraiou
Alice Labourel
Elie Lakin
Felipe Lanuza Rilling
Chris Leung
Ross Lovegrove
Lux
Hugh McEwen
Ryan Mehanna
Lucia Mondardini
Marianne Mulvey
Josef Musil
Ollie Palmer
Igor Pantic
Bakul Patki
Elliot Payne
Michael Pelken

Marco Poletto
Martina Presepi
Molly Price
Caroline Reid
Ivan Del Renzio
David Roberts
Richard Roberts
Jenny Sabin
Bob Sheil
Rob Slater
Catrina Stewart
Ben Tew
Theodoros Themistokleous
Martha Tsigkari
Tijl Vanmeirhaeghe
Filip Visnjic
Hugh Whitehead
Andrew Witt
Mellisa Woolford
Stefanie Wuschitz
Fiona Zisch

bartlett.ucl.ac.uk/architecture

Publisher
Bartlett School of Architecture, UCL

Editors
Frédéric Migayrou, Andrew Porter

Graphic Design
Patrick Morrissey, Unlimited
weareunlimited.co.uk

Editorial Coordination
Michelle Lukins, Laura Cherry

For more information on all the programmes and
modules at The Bartlett Faculty of the Built
Environment, UCL, visit bartlett.ucl.ac.uk

The Bartlett School of Architecture, UCL
Wates House
Gordon Street
London WC1H 0QB
T. +44 (0)20 7679 7504
F. +44 (0)20 7679 4831
architecture@ucl.ac.uk

ISBN 978-0-9572355-6-4